The Underground Railroad

A Captivating Guide to the Network of Routes, Places, and People in the United States That Helped Free African Americans during the Nineteenth Century

Free Bonus from Captivating History
(Available for a Limited time)

Hi History Lovers!

Now you have a chance to join our exclusive history list so you can get your first history ebook for free as well as discounts and a potential to get more history books for free! Simply visit the link below to join.

Captivatinghistory.com/ebook

Also, make sure to follow us on Facebook, Twitter and Youtube by searching for Captivating History.

Contents

The soul that is within me no man can degrade.

- Frederick Douglass

Introduction

The Underground Railroad wasn't underground. Nor was it a railroad. It was, however, an awe-inspiring piece of history, and one that speaks of hope even today.

Two hundred years ago, slavery had the Southern United States firmly in its evil grip. Around four million African Americans languished in the most appalling of living conditions, their lives controlled by people who saw them as objects. They were starved, whipped, and put to work despite being pregnant, sick, or so young that they could barely walk. They were despised, downtrodden, and degraded in every way. They longed for freedom, yet to reach the free land of Canada, they would have to cross thousands of miles filled with the threat of slave catchers, men who had made it their business to snatch desperate people who were on the very brink of liberty.

It was a hopeless time, but it was also a time of heroes. The only hope that these enslaved people had of escaping their brutal fates was the Underground Railroad. This fabled network of people and places delivered tens of thousands of escaped slaves all the way across the northern United States and into Canada. And while many of the people who made these escapes possible have melted away into history as faceless heroes, we know the names and stories of many. Their stories are some of the most inspiring that we will ever hear.

In this book, you will toil alongside the people who lived in bondage. You will witness the suffering of five-year-old Harriet Tubman, who was charged with caring for a slave owner's baby and whipped every time the infant cried. You will hear the fervent pleas of Benjamin Lay, the four-foot-high Quaker abolitionist whose eccentricities were far outweighed by his passionate heart for justice. You will feel the desperation of William Still, a man who was born free yet whose family was torn apart by slavery. And you will witness the incredible courage of each of these heroes as they joined hands to lead thousands of enslaved people to freedom.

The Underground Railroad is a testimony to what humanity's greatest can do in the face of its greatest depravity. And this is their story.

Chapter 1 – Slavery through the Ages

The story of slavery is a long and tragic one, and it reaches back further than many of us realize.

While the world only truly awoke to the pure evil of slavery in the 18th and 19th centuries, with tensions surrounding this issue reaching a boiling point in the United States in the middle of the 19th century, the abominable practice had been taking place for thousands of years by that point—over five thousand years, in fact, for slavery can be found in the earliest records of human history.

Slavery in the Ancient World

It's likely that slavery began around the Neolithic Period. Many people started to move away from the hunter-gatherer lifestyle that had previously sustained primitive tribes, and agriculture began to spread across the world. The rise of agriculture enabled humans to settle in larger and more stable villages and, later, cities. As the focus shifted away from sheer daily survival, hierarchies began to develop, cultures became more distinct from one another, and all the complexities of human society followed.

Slavery was one of them. Long before the first books were written or the first stone tablets inscribed, slaves were tilling the fields of their fellow man. The concept of some people being less important or less worthy than others likely arose during early history when the less intellectual Neanderthals walked the earth among the *Homo sapiens.*

Our first real record of slavery originates from 3500 BCE—more than 5,000 years ago. According to records from the ancient civilization of Sumer, which was located in modern-day Iraq, slavery had been around for hundreds of years by that point. The records insinuate that slavery had become a common fact of life.

As with most early slaves, the men and women who worked without freedom in Sumer were prisoners of war. Conflicts between tribes and cities gave rise to hundreds of prisoners, and it wasn't long before early leaders realized that these prisoners could be more useful alive than dead. In chains, these people were forced to work. Even then, slavery was fueled by the idea that the conquered people must be fundamentally inferior to the conquerors. It was no longer a case of *Homo sapiens* enslaving Neanderthals, but slaves were still considered to be different and thus inferior.

By the time of Sumer, enslaved people had become a reality of daily life. These were incidental prisoners of war, likely not the result of raids explicitly for the purpose of capturing people to enslave. The children of enslaved people were also automatically enslaved themselves. Merchants were involved in the trading of slaves, although it should be noted that the dedicated slave trader had not yet been invented.

This type of slavery—in which human beings are treated as possessions, with no rights whatsoever and can be bought, sold, and used in any way the owner pleases—is known as chattel slavery. It would continue to be practiced across most of the world, eventually giving rise to the Underground Railroad that this book seeks to explore.

Enslaved people became a part of almost every major civilization in the ancient world. Many of the ancient wonders were built by hands that spent much of their time in shackles. The glorious cities immortalized in ancient words were built, stone by stone, by men in chains. The gods that have passed from religion into mythology were served by prostitutes and other temple workers who had no voice, no say in their own lives, and no freedom. The ancient empires of Babylon, Greece, and Rome captured thousands of prisoners of war in their many conquests, and untold multitudes were enslaved.

A Brief Decline of Slavery in Europe

The fall of Rome marked the end of antiquity and the beginning of the Middle Ages. In some ways, when Rome fell, so did many of its ideas. While many of them, such as a form of democracy and advanced knowledge of subjects like mathematics, science, and literature, would be deeply missed during the Dark Ages, slavery was one Roman concept that the world could do without.

However, the exploitation of one human being by another was ever-present during the Middle Ages in Europe. Slavery was replaced by serfdom, which was hardly any better. The feudal system became commonplace throughout Europe, first in the west and then in the east, and serfs were at the very bottom of the pecking order. These people tilled the lands of the wealthy, and they often had little say in the work they would do; they also did not have equal rights as landowners. However, they had more freedoms than chattel slaves. Manumission was not only legal but also possible, as serfs were able to earn money. Many serfs chose not to buy their freedom, though, as their feudal lords provided them with protection. Instead, serfs bought land of their own. They owed their lords tax on this land, often in the form of a portion of the land's produce.

In times of war, serfs could also be recruited for the fyrd. The fyrd was a regiment of common soldiers in the Middle Ages, who usually only had a few weeks' training. A frugal lord would barely bother to supply armor for his fyrdmen, as they were often considered cannon fodder. Serfs had no real say in the matter—if their lord wanted them in the fyrd, they had to go whether they liked it or not.

Serfs also had little opportunity to improve their own lives. They were born into their occupations (a carpenter's son, for instance, would be trained to become a carpenter) and usually had little to no education. However, serfs were able to marry and to lead more or less normal family lives. This was a simple, vital freedom that was almost always denied to those in chattel slavery.

Serfs often lived downtrodden lives, and sometimes they were very badly treated by their lords, but there is an important distinction between serfdom and slavery. This exploitative practice would continue throughout Europe for hundreds of years. It faded from most of western Europe around the 16th century. In eastern Europe and Asia, it would continue for about another 300 years, finally being abolished in Russia in the 19th century.

Africa's Great Empires

After the fall of serfdom, Europe was by no means free of slavery. In fact, the end of serfdom ushered in an entirely new era, one in which slavery had never been more central to the history and the economy of the world. And the people who were enslaved in the millions during this time almost all came from one continent: Africa.

By the time of the transatlantic slave trade, which involved the ancestors of the enslaved people who would eventually use the Underground Railroad, Africa had already had a long and complicated history. Although European scholars of prior centuries had done much damage to the popular conception of African history, this continent was still home to some of the richest, most sophisticated, and most powerful empires in history. And when Spanish and Portuguese traders first began to sell human beings from Africa, slavery was by no means a new concept to the continent.

In fact, one of the oldest ancient civilizations to utilize enslaved people was Kemet, better known as ancient Egypt. Kemet became one of the most advanced civilizations of its time around 3000 BCE. Even 5,000 years later, the incredible constructions of this mighty society still stand; tourists flock to view the pyramids of Giza and the Sphinx every year. While the idea that the pyramids were built by enslaved people is likely a myth—latest research shows that the pyramids were probably built by compensated laborers, likely local farmers—slavery was still a reality of daily life in Kemet. Like citizens of other ancient civilizations, ancient Egyptians considered themselves fundamentally superior to other people. They primarily enslaved prisoners of war, but chattel slavery could also be a punishment to people who had failed to pay their debts or committed certain crimes.

In fact, during the time of ancient Egypt, it was not Europeans who enslaved Africans; there is evidence that ancient Egyptians may have had European slaves as well.

Kemet was not the only great civilization of ancient Africa, although it is perhaps the most well known. In countries that labor due to conflict and poverty in the modern day, massive empires once stood proud and ruled over vast stretches of the glorious African landscape. In Sudan, which is today torn apart by civil war, the mighty Kingdom of Kush once ruled. Located along the Cataracts of the Nile, three successive Kushite kingdoms built thriving cities and established an extensive trade network that stretched across Africa, the Middle East, and southern Europe and Asia. The Kingdom of Kush lasted from around 2500 BCE to around 300 CE—three times longer than the better-known empire of ancient Rome.

The Axum Empire was a shorter-lived power that still left its mark on African history. Existing between the 1st and 6th centuries CE, the Axum Empire encompassed an enormous tract of land, which included modern-day Ethiopia, Somaliland, Djibouti, Somali, and Eritrea. This was an educated empire, one of the first in the world to formally adopt Christianity. It also minted its own coins (a first for this part of Africa) and invented a script named Ge'ez, which is still in use to this day.

During the Late Middle Ages, another even larger power arose in Africa: the Mali Empire. Like the Kingdom of Kush, the Mali Empire was known for its amazing riches and extensive trade. It had strong connections with the Muslim powers of the Middle East, and its cities became known as enlightened centers for education. In fact, the Mali Empire was a progressive, forward-thinking state, employing concepts like democracy, which still eluded much of Europe.

Kush, Axum, and Mali were mighty empires, yet their names lack the familiar ring of names like Rome, Greece, and Macedonia. Sadly, during the era of the transatlantic slave trade, many historians made it their mission to utterly dehumanize Africans and convince Europeans that African people were inferior. Just like the ancient Egyptians and the ancient people of Sumer, Europeans of this time considered themselves to be the superior race. This tragically led to the loss of much of Africa's rich history. To this day, African history is less well known to the Western world than the histories of Europe and North America.

Slavery of Africans

While there were many grand empires across the African continent, much of its population lived in smaller societies. These rich, colorful cultures often practiced a form of democracy long before the concept ever reached Europe. In these smaller societies, people generally lived in freedom, often with powerful traditions, close family ties, and intricate beliefs deeply connected to the natural world surrounding them. To this day, many of these traditions endure in indigenous African populations, making this continent culturally diverse.

However, in the larger states, slavery was a common fact of life long before traders shipped enslaved Africans across the Atlantic. Like Kemet, ancient African empires practiced many different types of slavery. Some people were only enslaved temporarily to work off a debt or endure a sentence for their crimes. Others were chattel slaves. The exportation of these enslaved people began long before Christopher Columbus ever set eyes on the New World. Africans sold their enslaved counterparts to various different countries, most notably the Muslim powers of the Middle East, as well as to Asia.

The Transatlantic Slave Trade

The transatlantic slave trade was, by far, the largest exportation of human beings out of Africa, and it was responsible for massive depopulation and a devastating economic effect on the continent. It was unlike anything Africa had ever seen before.

As early as Columbus's arrival in the New World, slaves were already being exported from Africa to the Mediterranean by Spanish and Portuguese merchants. Once small colonies were established on the Caribbean islands in the early 16th century, it was only natural for Portuguese and Spanish settlers to bring Africans as slaves, adding to the force of enslaved indigenous peoples already toiling under European whips on the islands. After that, the African slaves spread as quickly as Europeans did.

The slave trade was originally controlled almost exclusively by the Spanish and, in particular, the Portuguese. In fact, the first enslaved Africans to be brought to North America were shipped by the Spanish, not the British. In 1619, a handful of Spanish merchant vessels traveled across the Atlantic, bringing wares—including people—from Africa to the Spanish colonies of Central and South America. They were ambushed by a bunch of British pirates that summer. The Spanish were overwhelmed, and the triumphant British returned to their colony of Jamestown, Virginia, in August 1619 with the booty. Among the loot was a small group of terrified people: twenty African men, women, and children. These people had already been forcibly removed from their homes in Africa, forced onto slave ships, and then taken across the perilous Atlantic, a long voyage endured under awful conditions. Then they listened to the sounds of battle as the

English defeated the Spanish. Perhaps they even hoped that these new people would free them or even just treat them with respect.

Their hopes were cruelly dashed. The twenty Africans were put to work in the tobacco fields of Virginia, and they would spend the rest of their lives in bondage.

Like most African people exported to the Americas, these original twenty originated from West Africa. Sadly, they were possibly captured by other Africans. The slave trade had been a reality in Africa for centuries before Europeans ever arrived there, and when Portuguese and Spanish traders first started poking around for slaves to export, some African nations were all too happy to sell them their prisoners of war at a premium price. As the demand for enslaved people increased, so did the supply, with some African nations turning on one another to capture hundreds of people simply to sell. It was also not unusual for Europeans to invade African towns and villages and kidnap people directly.

A few parts of Africa managed to avoid being part of the slave trade. While West Africa was very hard hit, most southern African peoples never partook in slavery themselves and were appalled that the Europeans wanted to buy people from them. The Xhosa of modern-day South Africa is an example of a free people who refused to engage in the slave trade.

Once the people had been captured, either by African warlords or European traders, they had to be taken all the way to the ports on the west coast of Africa. This was a grueling journey in itself. Ripped away from their families and homes, surrounded by unfamiliar people speaking a strange language, tied up, abused, and stripped of all their rights, these people were forced to make the journey on foot. Traders were hasty, wanting to sell the people as quickly as possible to the captains of slavers. They cared little for anyone who was injured or fell ill on the way. Around 10 percent of people perished before they even reached the ships.

However, those who did reach the slavers' ships would find that their terrible trials were only just beginning. The route across the Atlantic to the Americas became known as the Middle Passage, and the terrors these people endured aboard those ships were some of the worst ordeals that mankind has ever faced.

Already exhausted, traumatized, and weakened from the long journey they'd just endured, the captives now found themselves being handed over to yet another gang of rough strangers. Nothing would be explained to them—they were less than human in the eyes of the slave traders. Here, couples would be separated, children taken from their families. People who had been married for decades would be torn apart, while little children were pulled from their mother's arms. In the chaos, people would be shackled and forced to board the ships. Some of these people had never even seen the ocean before, and many had never seen ships. They were dragged on board into the unknown, and the unknown would be far worse than they could have imagined.

Slave ships were built for just one thing: to carry as many people as possible, regardless of the welfare of their human cargo. Some could carry 400 people or more. The only way this was possible was to cram people into the ships in astoundingly crowded conditions. The space each person was allowed was coffin-like in its proportions. They were forced to lie down, often wearing iron shackles that chafed the skin and caused raw wounds. Their beds were nothing but wooden planks, and suppurating sores formed on these hapless people, who were often unable to turn onto their sides. Stacked two or three deep, their noses mere inches from the roof of their space, these people had to endure utter darkness and the buck and sway of the ship as it crossed the perilous Atlantic. Seasickness was inevitable. Vomit was left where it lay.

Female captives were at even more of a disadvantage. Sailors were discouraged from sexually abusing their charges since they needed to be kept in as good a condition as was economically viable in order to sell their cargo for a high price in the New World, but it still happened.

Rations were appallingly poor for these captives. Even at the best of times, they were often given just enough to keep them alive until they reached the New World; should something go wrong and rations began to run low before they reached port, sailors would immediately cut the captives' rations, allowing them to starve. The enslaved were allowed on deck at times but only for a few hours and only in small, subdued groups. Any attempt at rebellion was immediately met with savage violence from the sailors. Mutiny by slaves was something that all slave traders feared, but it was seldom successful; suicide, on the other hand, became common. Many captives chose death in the turbulent sea rather than the terrible unknown.

Life as a Slave in the United States

The enslaved people who made it all the way to the New World would find themselves utterly at the mercy of the people who bought, sold, and traded them as if they were pieces of furniture.

Slavery had been legal throughout all of the colonies. After the American Revolution, the new US Constitution made an allowance for slavery. Slavery ended up being relegated to the Southern states (although northern states still kept slaves for a period of time), but this did not seem to impede its growth. Hundreds of thousands—and later as many as four million—enslaved people lived, suffered, and toiled in many different roles throughout the American South. Some of these were highly skilled tradesmen who might otherwise have built themselves a prosperous life; others were illiterate souls who knew little other than picking cotton.

Either way, none of them had easy lives. The world into which the captives on the slave ships were brought was one in which slavery had become an immovable institution, a part of the economy, of society, and of life. Enslaved people were status symbols; they were seen as essential for business and thus became a significant part of the economy. What they were not, in the eyes of their captors, was human. This was immediately evident in the way an enslaved person was treated upon arrival in the New World.

Once slave traders brought their "wares" to US ports, their first order of business was to sell them as soon as possible. These sick, malnourished people, often with festering sores on their bodies from the inhumane conditions in which they had been transported, would have to be made presentable. No privacy was afforded to them. They were stripped naked and washed. Oil was rubbed into their open wounds, not to heal them but to hide them. Some slaves were even branded with a blazing hot iron pressed into their skin. Then they were separated into holding pens like unlucky cattle. Families were torn apart, as young men went into one pen, young women into the other, with screaming children ripped from the arms of their mothers. It was a world of utter chaos, ruled over by the lash of the slavers, and there was no escape.

Their fates were then decided by the fall of the hammer. Men gathered around to bid on various slaves, buying them as casually as one would buy a cuckoo clock or an old sofa. They would then be taken to their new homes—homes where they would know little other than hard labor and aching want.

Since these people were traveling through a new world full of unfamiliar people, animals, crops, and landscapes, they must have been unbelievably terrified. Sadly, some slave owners were worse than anything these slaves could have imagined.

While some slaves lived in tolerable conditions and were treated with a measure of kindness by the people who saw them as their property, other enslaved people, particularly those who worked in the fields, had utterly terrible lives. African children could be sent to work in the tobacco or cotton fields when they were as young as six years old. Old people did not work in the cotton fields simply because enslaved people did not grow old. The terrible conditions under which they worked, combined with poor diets and the lack of medical care, often led to early deaths. The average life expectancy of an African slave in the United States when slavery was at its height was just thirty-six years.

Every day was a struggle. Enslaved people were woken early, as their overseers prevented them from sleeping for too long, believing that a lack of sleep would keep them subdued and less likely to rebel. They were sent out into the fields to work in the blistering sun, picking cotton that often tore and blistered their fingers. Overseers made sure that no enslaved person took a break or worked too slowly. Meals were sparse and of poor nutritional quality. Their houses were not so much homes as they were shacks or barns, better suited for sheep or cattle.

Education was out of the question for almost all enslaved people. In fact, it was against the law for Africans to be taught how to read or write. They could not testify in court against a white person, and there was almost no penalty for the rape of an African woman. Masters could do with their women as they pleased, and if a non-slave owner raped an African woman, he could only be charged at worst with trespass. After all, these women were not considered humans but property.

However, the punishments for enslaved people were appalling. They could be whipped so severely that scars would be left on their backs for the rest of their lives. The withholding of food or water was not against the law.

These people lived short, agonizing lives after their arrival in the New World, and even when the transatlantic slave trade was abolished in the US in 1808, it was, by no means, an end to slavery in the country. Enslaved people fell in love and got married, although their marriages were not legally recognized. Their children were by default the property of their mother's master, and some masters even encouraged enslaved women to become pregnant, knowing that they could tear the children from their mothers' arms and sell them for a good price. So, the enslaved population in the US continued to grow unabated, even though shipping people across the Atlantic was now illegal. In addition, people continued to be shipped across the Middle Passage until just before the American Civil War broke out.

As for Africa itself, it would be horrendously impacted by the constant plunder of its people. A total of around twenty-five million Africans were exported as slaves, both to the New World and to the Middle East, during the transatlantic slave trade. The effect on Africa's population was such that the total population of the entire continent failed to grow for a long period. In fact, it declined, as did Africa's economy. Without those millions of people, who could have become farmers, politicians, warriors, tradesmen, merchants, sailors, scholars, or spiritual leaders, Africa's economic growth stalled. Moreover, the use of African Americans as slaves led most European and New World powers to view Africans themselves as inherently inferior, even more so than before the slave trade. Therefore, they were far more likely to conquer and colonize African countries rather than enter into trade with them.

Unbelievably, though, there was a light at the end of the tunnel. Even though slavery had spread all over the world, it was an evil that would ultimately be conquered (at least legally), even though the fight looked utterly hopeless at first. And it was an evil that would be conquered by some of history's most fearless heroes: abolitionists.

Chapter 2 – Abolition around the World

A 19th-century lithograph of Queen Nzinga Mbande.

https://commons.wikimedia.org/wiki/File:Ann_Zingha.jpg

Slavery had been an almost immovable institution for centuries by the time the Middle Ages receded and the Age of Enlightenment dawned. With this movement came new ideas, such as new thoughts on freedom, which included freedom from bondage. By the late 17th century, a new social movement was rising against slavery, and its name was abolitionism.

Before abolitionism ever had a name, there were scattered and courageous efforts to stand against slavery. One of these took place in Africa itself.

An African Queen and Her Free Country

Long before suffering Africans would be shipped across the brutal Middle Passage to work in the cotton fields of the Deep South, there were already people advocating against the idea of slavery.

One of the most notable African voices against slavery belonged to a female ruler, one of many powerful queens who would reign over various parts of the continent, whose list includes the biblical Queen of Sheba and Cleopatra of Egypt. This queen's name is not as well known today, but she was a force to be reckoned with during her time.

Queen Nzinga Mbande ruled over a small group of Mbundu people, having ascended to the throne in 1624 following the death of her brother. Her kingdom was a peaceful one—or at least it had been until the Portuguese came. Ndongo was located near modern-day Luanda, the capital city of Angola in southern Africa. Centuries before it would be torn apart in the Border War during the Cold War-era, Angola was already being ravaged by Portuguese colonists. They had been trying to control various African states ever since the 15th century, as they saw Africa as a breeding ground for people to enslave. Humans were one of the most valuable items that Portugal could trade, and there was an abundance of people to enslave in Africa, people whom most colonists considered to be inferior simply because of their skin color and culture.

Many Africans were quick to make allies of the Portuguese and started to sell their fellow countrymen to slave traders. Wars burst out across the continent, as African allies of European powers began to plunder their neighbors for prisoners of war who could be sold as slaves. Terrible raids were conducted on innocent villagers, who would find themselves being carried off, regardless of gender or age, by other Africans. Ndongo was horribly affected, and when Queen Nzinga took power, she found herself ruling over a country that was being plundered of the most valuable resource of all: humanity.

Desperate to save her country, Queen Nzinga's first thought was to become an ally of the Portuguese. As much as the slave trade had detestably affected her people, Queen Nzinga knew she didn't have the military power to start a war against them or to defend Ndongo from the raiders who so frequently came within its borders to carry off its people. This seemed to work. For two years, there was a tentative peace between Ndongo and Portugal, and the raids decreased for a time. But in 1626, the Portuguese turned on Nzinga, breaking their alliance without a second thought.

Betrayed and beaten, Nzinga had nowhere left to turn, and she was beleaguered on every side by colonists and raiders. So, she did the unthinkable. She packed up her entire country and left.

Accompanied by many of her people, Nzinga started a trek west, fleeing with her subjects across hostile terrain in a bid to escape the far-reaching impact of the Portuguese. She only stopped when she reached Matamba. This area had been home to some Mbundu people for decades, but it was only loosely governed. It wasn't long before Nzinga conquered those few Matambans who resisted her and became the queen of Ndongo and Matamba.

Now that she was safely out of the reach of the Portuguese—and of her new rival back in Ndongo—Nzinga was finally able to take the stand she'd always wanted. She began to openly fight against slavery, opening Matamba's borders as a sanctuary to all runaway slaves. With West Africa being so harshly affected by slavery, Matamba became a place of refuge, and runaway slaves flocked to join Nzinga's land of freedom.

The increase in population and, thus, military power quickly made Matamba into a much larger and more important kingdom than Ndongo had been. By the end of Nzinga's reign, Matamba was no longer simply another population of largely helpless Africans that the Portuguese could plunder at will. Instead, it was a vast and well-respected kingdom that engaged in trade with its neighboring nations. Eventually, Matamba became a center of trade in West Africa, and it even traded plentifully with Portugal itself. The Portuguese found themselves on an equal footing with Matamba and were unable to take any of its people as slaves.

Abolition in the British Empire

Shortly after the rule of Queen Nzinga, the idea of abolishing slavery began to spread. The Age of Enlightenment had brought new ideas to the world. Thinking began to change, and people started to value freedom more than ever.

Freedom was a little-known concept in much of the 17th-century world, far from the centerpiece of modern morality that it has become today. At that time, most people were not free to choose their careers, believe as they pleased, or even choose their rulers. Absolute monarchy was the norm, and religious freedom was almost unheard of. Even one's occupation was decided, usually by one's parents, just as their occupations had been decided by their parents.

But change began to sweep across the world. In the 16th and 17th centuries, the rise of Protestantism challenged one of Europe's oldest institutions: the Roman Catholic Church. The French and American Revolutions of the late 18th century showed that monarchies were no longer wholly accepted. In fact, many important countries began to utterly reject it and embraced the idea of democracy.

While the idea of freedom grew across the world, slavery grew as well. Even though man became more attracted to freedom, he continued to take it from his fellows. Slavery continued to grow steadily during the Enlightenment, but that age still engendered the ideas that would finally bring it to an end.

Slavery proliferated in the Deep South, but Southerners were by no means the only guilty parties. The British Empire witnessed a stunning zenith during this time, and while slavery was rare in England itself, it was absolutely rife in its many colonies, which included South Africa, Australia, India, Canada, and the Caribbean. The enormous variety of agriculture and other industries being practiced across the British Empire were fueled by the labor of enslaved people; about 3.1 million Africans were dragged from their homes to work in the British Empire's many territories.

Even though the economy of England itself was not as dependent upon slavery as that of its colonies, enslaved Africans were still present in Britain. Merchants, lords, civil servants, and other wealthy British people who had been to the colonies would often bring their slaves with them, as they were used to the convenience of owning another human being. These slaves would sometimes stay and serve the family, but sometimes they would end up being sold back to the colonies, which was a terrible fate, akin to a second Middle Passage for people who had already endured so much.

One such enslaved person was named Jonathan Strong, and in 1765, he managed to displease his master in some way or another. His master laid into him with a whip—an all-too-common punishment—and laid his back open in terrible red scars. Strong didn't know it at the time, but his beating would turn the tide of slavery in the United Kingdom (and in the British Empire) forever.

Strong had befriended a thirty-year-old British civil servant named Granville Sharp. An avid musician and theologian, Sharp was dismayed by the terrible treatment of Strong, and he was even unhappier when Strong's master decided that he would simply sell his errant slave back to people in the Caribbean.

Sharp couldn't comprehend how such a dreadful thing could be permissible in a country that was supposed to pride itself on its lawfulness. He opened a case against Strong's owner. Going to the lord mayor himself, Sharp petitioned for Strong to be released, and against the odds, he succeeded in his efforts for justice to be served. Strong became a free man in England, and in 1772, Sharp succeeded in pushing through a ruling that forbade any enslaved person from being forced to return to the colonies after coming to Britain.

While it was still legal for enslaved people to be owned in Britain, and although slavery continued freely throughout the British colonies, this was a big step forward. Most owners abandoned the use of enslaved people within Britain itself. No more would there be African men and women in chains on this island, but the fight was a long way from won. Sharp was well aware of that, and he sought to pass on his fever for abolition to those who would follow in his footsteps.

Unfortunately, Sharp's position as a civil servant did not last for long. He resigned in 1776, appalled by the bloodshed that the British Empire was wreaking in America during the American Revolutionary War. However, he was a long way from done, and he joined with a new ally to work harder for the freedom of Africans throughout the British Empire.

This new ally was named Thomas Clarkson. Twenty-five years Sharp's junior, Clarkson had been an abolitionist since the tender age of nineteen. He was studying at Cambridge when he decided to enter a competition for essays written in Latin. Clarkson, then already troubled by the prospect of people working in chains within the empire he loved, chose slavery as the topic for his essay in 1779.

The essay was a wonderful success. Even though it was fairly anti-slavery in tone, as it explored the lawfulness of slavery, it won the competition, and for six years, Clarkson was excited by this prestigious achievement. However, one day in 1785, as he was riding to London, Clarkson was overcome by a sudden melancholy. As his horse strode along under a summer sky, its rider grew increasingly troubled as he pondered not the success of his essay, nor its accolades, but its contents.

Clarkson realized how unfair it was that some people were being forced to labor in the colonies that made Britain so wealthy, while he was allowed to live a free life with an education, to win prizes, and to write anything he liked. The thought was enough that he brought his horse to a halt, dismounted, and indulged in his thoughts. When he got back onto the horse, he was fully committed to the abolition of slavery.

Clarkson's first move was to translate his essay into English and publish it so that more readers would be able to access his ideas. It was widely read, and many people found it deeply challenging. Of course, many rich and powerful men utterly rejected his ideas, but abolitionists flocked to him for his willingness to speak out on the issue of slavery. One such was Granville Sharp. The men quickly became fast friends, and in 1787, they formed the Committee for the Abolition of the African Slave Trade.

Neither man, however, held much political punch. They would need a far higher-ranking person to join them in order to have any real effect on the law, especially considering that Sharp was no longer a civil servant. The man who joined them became the face of abolition in the British Empire: William Wilberforce.

Wilberforce would have been an unlikely candidate if Sharp and Clarkson had approached him a few years earlier. After a misspent youth, in which he was far more interested in drinking and carousing until late into the night than he was in his education, Wilberforce had taken up a career in politics. Motivated only by his own pride and vanity, Wilberforce worked hard to prove himself, despite his ulterior motives. He became a member of Parliament in 1780 at the age of twenty-one.

After five years in this position, Wilberforce found that he was tired of his empty life. His selfishness had earned him popularity and power, and his wealth had earned him all the booze and entertainment he could ever want, yet none of this could make him happy anymore. The same year that Clarkson sat by the roadside pondering abolition, Wilberforce sank into a deep, deep depression.

This shroud of sorrow would only be lifted months later. During the Easter of 1786, Wilberforce found himself crawling out of the hole, and he was not the same he had once been. Wilberforce was a changed man now, a man who believed that God had a divine purpose for his life. Thanks to the influence of Clarkson, who had been looking for a powerful politician to champion their cause in Parliament, Wilberforce had become an abolitionist. His life was no longer purposeless; now, he had an all-consuming passion that would occupy the remainder of his days.

Clarkson and Wilberforce both served on the Committee for the Abolition of the African Slave Trade, and they each had a specific role. Clarkson sought evidence against slavery so he could show the civilized British how brutally their slave traders had been treating their fellow humankind. He even obtained slaving equipment from the slave ships, such as shackles and other awful, inhumane restraints. Wilberforce brought these into Parliament and pled the cause of enslaved Africans, petitioning for abolition throughout the British Empire.

He was optimistic the first time. Perhaps even the second and the third. But as bill after bill failed to pass Parliament, Wilberforce's health began to suffer. He withstood numerous bouts of crippling illness that often confined him to his room. Appalled by the inaction of Parliament, Wilberforce tried to continue working through his pain, and he was prescribed opium to help. At the time, no one knew that opium was deadly addictive, and Wilberforce, who had managed to shake off his addiction to alcohol, soon found himself irretrievably in the grip of opium.

However, his addiction did not dim his purpose. Fighting against the odds, Wilberforce attempted nine times to get an anti-slavery bill through Parliament. When his tenth bill was presented in 1833, he was on his deathbed, barely able to move. But the tenth time was the charm. The bill went through at last, and while it would be decades before slavery was abolished by the majority of countries, the first great step had been taken.

Wilberforce lived just long enough to see his bill succeed at last. He died three days after receiving the news.

Clarkson's story ended more happily. Not only did he live to see slavery almost completely abolished throughout the British Empire by the Slavery Abolition Act of 1833, but he also enjoyed a long and peaceful retirement in the village of Ipswich. He died there in 1846.

The British Empire was now a free one (except for a few pockets), and a few decades later, France followed its example in 1848. Two massive world powers had relinquished their hold on the "right" to enslave people, but another great power, the United States, still clung on stubbornly. Yet the first rumbles of abolition were already shaking the US, and the Southern slave owners would not be unopposed for long. And a certain religious group would prove to be a key part of the abolition movement there, just as it had been in Britain.

Chapter 3 – Abolition in the United States

William Williams's 1790 painting depicting Benjamin Lay.

https://commons.wikimedia.org/wiki/File:Benjamin_Lay_painted_by_William_Wil liams_in_1790.jpg

Some of America's very first abolitionists made their stand long before abolition began in the British Empire. In fact, they were instrumental in abolition efforts in Britain as well, but the US was a vital part of their history as a religious group.

The Religious Society of Friends was formed in the 17th century, a time of much religious upheaval for the Reformation had begun to take hold across Europe (and drive countless Europeans, especially British, to populate the New World and form profoundly Protestant colonies). The Anglican Church had broken away from the Roman Catholic Church, yet it retained many of its strict religious laws. The Protestants formed a much-persecuted church of their own, one with far fewer regulations and trappings than the Anglican and Catholic Churches.

However, even the Protestants had a structured hierarchy, something that chafed at the morality of George Fox, an Englishman. He believed that God was present in every living thing and that there was no need for clergy to lead people to God but that everyone could experience God via "the inner light." This led him to form the Religious Society of Friends, which was angrily called the "Quakers" by many others. They would eventually adopt this once-derogatory term, and today, they are better known by this nickname.

Almost immediately, the Quakers faced persecution in the land of their birth: England. They were rejected by Protestants and Anglicans alike, and like the Protestants, they fled to a new world that held the promise of a new beginning. After arriving in North America, the Quakers soon discovered that it was no utopia. The Protestants had already begun to form their own idea of paradise there, and this included rejecting non-Protestants. Just as they themselves had been persecuted in the Old World, the Protestants now persecuted the Quakers. Some were executed and brutally killed.

Still, the Quakers hung on, eventually forming a thriving colony in Pennsylvania, among others. The group grew and ultimately flourished despite persecution. Soon it began to lay down more concrete rules, and meetings were held to discuss a variety of issues. One of these issues was slavery. In the late 17ᵗʰ century, abolition was still very much a thing of the future, as the institution of slavery was a deeply rooted part of life in all of the colonies. The Quakers became one of the first religious groups to declare slavery immoral at a meeting in 1688.

This did not prevent Quakers from owning slaves. Many Quakers ignored this proclamation, at least in the beginning, and continued to profit from the slaves they owned. For decades, no action was taken against them. But the first Quaker who took real action against slavery was born even before slavery was declared immoral, and despite his small stature, this man would make a big difference.

Benjamin Lay was born in England to Quaker parents, and he took up the faith avidly in his youth. To all appearances, he had been born disadvantaged. Not only was he a member of a marginalized religious group, but Lay may have also suffered from dwarfism. He was recorded as being only four feet high and hunchbacked. However, this didn't stop him from following his dreams. Disliking his apprenticeship to a glover, Lay decided to abandon life in England at the age of twenty-one. He left his family behind to sail the open seas.

This opened up a whole new world for Lay. Back in rural England, there were nearly no slaves at all; most slave owners in England were wealthy people who had traveled to the colonies. Out on the seas, however, things were different. Sailors told him stories about their exploits on the slave ships and about the unspeakable suffering of those who were taken across the Middle Passage against their will.

If Lay had found these accounts difficult to believe, he would soon have no choice but to believe them, for he became an eyewitness to some of slavery's greatest horrors. After sailing for a time, he spent a while living in Barbados, which was then a British colony. Here, slavery was a part of everyday life. Thousands of African slaves toiled in its vast sugar plantations, and their lives were absolutely appalling.

Lay saw people suffering without medical care, without proper nutrition, without dignity, and without any of the most basic human rights. He saw people being savagely punished for the tiniest of transgressions or simply because of their masters' moods. Once, he saw an enslaved person who had been terribly beaten faced with the threat of yet another thrashing. The man couldn't comprehend another round of beating and took his own life instead.

All of these awful events felt utterly irreconcilable with what Lay had always been taught, that God existed in all human beings. He'd been taught about love and freedom, and yet all he saw was hatred and imprisonment. His mind was made up. Slavery was evil.

Lay returned to England, where he fell in love and married Sarah Smith, who also may have suffered from dwarfism. For ten years, Lay lived in a country where he rarely saw enslaved people, but he was already frustrated with his church. He often confronted his fellow Quakers during their meetings about all kinds of issues, especially targeting the wealthy and worldly. This resulted in numerous expulsions from Quaker groups, but loyal Sarah always stayed with him.

By 1732, Sarah and Benjamin Lay were both tired of life in England. They decided to move to Philadelphia, Pennsylvania, where they were faced with an appalling reality that Lay thought he had left behind in Barbados. At the time, Pennsylvania was absolutely rife with slavery. Nearly everyone owned at least one slave to tend livestock and work in their homes, and to Lay's utter disgust, this included many of his fellow Quakers. He could not understand why those who professed to believe the same things that he did would keep their fellow human beings in shackles.

At once, Lay began to cause the same kind of trouble in Philadelphia that had gotten him thrown out of his church back in England. He spoke up at numerous Quaker meetings, angrily accusing those who owned slaves of being the servants of Satan himself. Of course, many of these Quakers were well-respected and wealthy members of the community, and they did not take kindly to these harsh accusations. While some people did have the odd objection toward slavery, Lay's stance of disowning the entire institution as being immoral and even demonic was a unique one.

Lay was hugely dedicated to this cause, often planning elaborate demonstrations and using visual aids to try to force his audience to understand what he was saying. One time, he brought tobacco pipes into a meeting and broke them, tossing the pieces into the rows of assembled Quakers, shouting his accusations. It wasn't long before Lay earned the reputation of being a hopeless eccentric.

Three years after their arrival in Philadelphia, tragedy struck, as Sarah Lay died in 1735. Benjamin Lay was utterly shattered, and a second blow came shortly after her death when he was formally disowned by the Religious Society of Friends for his strange behavior, a decision that was influenced, no doubt, by the wealthy slave owners who disliked being called out on something they found so profitable.

Neither hardship could sway Lay's conviction when it came to the subject of slavery. He continued to protest slavery in Quaker meetings despite his disowning, and his protests became more and more dramatic. The most dramatic of all occurred in 1738 at an important assembly in New Jersey. Lay was an unassuming little figure at first, his small body swaddled in a huge greatcoat as the meeting began. But when he had a chance to speak, he became larger than life, his voice booming around the building as he accused the gathered slave owners of their sin.

When he cast off the greatcoat, the assembled Quakers were shocked to see that he was wearing a military uniform and a sword. Not only did he proclaim that slavery was evil, but he also asserted that all people were equal regardless of race—an almost unheard-of idea in 18th-century America. Growing more and more agitated, he condemned the actions of slave owners. He shouted, "Thus shall God shed the blood of those persons who enslave their fellow creatures!" Dramatically producing a book from his coat and drawing his sword, he thrust the blade through the covers of the book. To the horror of everyone watching, bright red liquid squirted out of the book and splattered all over Lay and everyone closest to him. He continued shouting and shaking "blood" over the other Quakers.

The liquid was not blood. It was just pokeberry juice. Lay was deeply against the killing of any living creature. In fact, after this demonstration, he retreated from society and built himself a little cave-like home in the wilderness. He refused to eat meat or eggs, subsisting only on plants and some milk. However, his abolitionist work was not finished. That same year, he finished writing his book, All Slave-Keepers That Keep the Innocent in Bondage, Apostates, which was one of the first literary works to truly condemn slavery. Lay called slavery not only immoral but also evil and ungodly.

As one might expect, the book was not well received. Neither was Lay; he would live out his days as something of a hermit, rejected by his own people. But his words had not gone completely unheard. Over the next two decades, change began to come over the Quakers. Although Lay died in 1759, he was able to hear that the first proper step toward the abolition of slavery among the Quakers had been taken. *HIS BOOK WOULD LATER BECOME WIDELY READ AMONG ANTI-SLAVERY SOCIETIES LATER IN THE CENTURY.*

It took the quakers nearly forty years, but they eventually heeded the words of lay and other quaker abolitionists. In 1774, they became one of the first religious groups to completely abolish slavery amongst themselves. Any quaker who continued to keep slaves would be disowned. Six years later, a largely quaker organization, the society for the protection of free negroes held in bondage (also known as the pennsylvania abolition society), succeeded in abolishing slavery in pennsylvania.

Abolition Begins in the United States

Although Benjamin Lay was already an abolitionist in the early 18th century, it would be many more decades before abolition became a nationwide issue in the United States. The idea of abolition actually took root in America around the same time slavery was being abolished in the British Empire.

After the American Revolutionary War, the US Constitution was created. It allowed for slavery, but many people were deeply discontented by this. They had so recently suffered great oppression from the British; to them, it seemed wrong that they would now continue to oppress others. The Second Great Awakening also contributed to the change of heart that was spreading across America. In the 18th and early 19th centuries, this Protestant revival sparked a new flood of religious zeal across the United States, and many people began to see slavery for what it was: a crime against humankind.

Another contributing factor to the early American abolition movement was the economy. In the North, keeping slaves just wasn't as profitable as it used to be. With immigrants from the overpopulated Old World flooding into the North, providing cheap labor and working to eke out small businesses of their own, slavery was no longer essential to the Northern economy. One state after the other began to abolish slavery until, by 1804, every state north of Maryland was free.

In the South, however, things were very different. The invention of the cotton gin—a machine for separating cotton seeds and fibers—had changed the whole landscape and economy of the South. Cotton had always been popular for making fabric, but the manual process of separating the seeds and fibers had made it uneconomical, and tobacco was a far more popular crop. The cotton gin made cotton processing exponentially cheaper, and suddenly, everyone with cotton plantations was making a vast amount of money.

However, picking cotton would be mechanized much later. This still had to be performed by hand, and the wealthy plantation owners weren't about to start paying somebody to do it. These large plantation owners possessed hundreds of enslaved people, and utilizing them instead of paid workers meant the owners only had to spend enough money to keep their slaves alive. Soon the entire economy of the South was built upon the cotton industry, and that, in turn, was built upon the bent and toiling backs of Africans in bondage.

A divide began to grow between the North and South, as the Northern states grew more and more resistant to slavery. By 1808, the importation of slaves had been made illegal in the United States. Although it was against the law to transport Africans on the Middle Passage, millions of them still suffered in the cotton fields, and the illegal smuggling of enslaved people from Africa to America would continue until around the time the American Civil War broke out.

One person who was key to the abolition of the slave trade was William Lloyd Garrison. Although his family was fabulously wealthy when he was born in 1805, Garrison knew plenty of want by the time he was a teenager. The 1807 Embargo Act, which placed strict restrictions on trade between the United States and the Old World, robbed Garrison's family of their finery, as it caused the US economy to crash. By the time Garrison was thirteen years old, his family could no longer pay his school fees. He started to work for newspapers in Massachusetts in a bid to pay his way through his education. Instead, Garrison stumbled into the calling that would define the rest of his years.

In 1826, at the tender age of nineteen, Garrison became the assistant editor of an abolitionist newspaper named the *Genius of Universal Emancipation*. The fire of abolition was quickly lit within him, and he started to grow more and more passionate about this cause. After numerous abortive attempts to start his own newspaper, he finally succeeded in 1831, starting his famous newspaper, *The Liberator*. This paper would run weekly for more than thirty years, and it became instrumental in the abolition of which Garrison dreamed.

The fact that *The Liberator* was widely read in the North pointed to a simple fact: Northerners were growing more and more critical of the institution of slavery. However, the wealthy South wasn't about to give up its booming economy. Instead, most Southerners started to find excuses for keeping slaves. They fell back on the old argument that Africans were inherently inferior to whites, saying that black people could never possibly care for themselves (even though they had been doing so in Africa for millennia and had built thriving societies and some of the ancient world's wealthiest, most educated nations). They also called slavery a "benevolent institution," saying that Africans could only survive thanks to the slave owners that fed and clothed them.

Even the Northerners, who were still largely racist, although they opposed slavery, could see that this was completely untrue. Their strong opinions against slavery began to spread into the South, and in the early 19ᵗʰ century, small groups of Southerners began to discuss and support the idea of emancipation. In fact, slavery might have ended decades before the Civil War if it wasn't for one desperate slave's violent bid for freedom in 1831, the same year that *The Liberator* was first published.

Nat Turner's Rebellion

Nathaniel Turner, better known as Nat, had suffered as cruelly as any of his brothers and sisters. Throughout his life, Turner had been bought, sold, beaten, and forced to do the whim of whatever master had purchased him.

Born in 1800 on a Virginia plantation owned by Benjamin Turner, Nat Turner might have been considered one of the lucky ones. He was given a basic education and became literate—something that was forbidden for most enslaved people.

Reading could have been considered a gift. To Turner, it became something he considered to be a holy burden. He wanted to share his gift with everyone, to spread ideas that had been denied his brothers and sisters in chains for so many generations. He became a preacher, and wherever he went, people were inspired by his words.

Considering that Turner was sold three times and hired out at least once, he came into contact with a large number of enslaved people. Their plight—and his own—convinced him that his people had to be led to freedom and that he was the one who had to do it. Looking around, he realized emancipation would never become a reality if it was left up to those in power in the South. He believed that freedom would never be given to Africans. Instead, they had to rise up and take it—at whatever cost.

In the 1820s, Turner found himself working on yet another plantation for yet another slave owner who didn't care for the hundreds of human beings that he owned. John Travis and his family exploited many Africans in their business, and Turner quickly became popular with the other enslaved people. They began to plan a rebellion against their master. Turner hoped that by overthrowing his own master, he might be able to find a way to free more Africans all over the South. Perhaps they could join forces with the North and put an end to slavery forever.

By the time the rebellion broke out, Turner was already thirty-one, and he knew that he didn't have much time left. The average life expectancy for enslaved people was only thirty-six; he was an old man by slave standards. Turner had planned the rebellion for years, but in 1831, he finally put it into action. A dramatic solar eclipse occurred early that year, and Turner took this to be a divine omen that it was time for him to eclipse the slave owners' power in Virginia.

His plan was put into action on August 21st, 1831. Together with six other enslaved men from his inner circle—although many others were in on the rebellion—Turner made for the elegant plantation home of the Travis family. They were sound asleep, and they would never wake again, for Turner and his men killed them all. Panic broke out on the plantation, and in the chaos, seventy-five more enslaved people broke their bonds and rushed out to join Turner in his bid for freedom. Fifty-five white Americans were killed in the chaos before Turner and his band fled into the Virginian countryside and hid.

They remained in hiding for several tense weeks. Slave owners were terrified of suffering the same gruesome fate as the Travis family, and they began to treat the people they had enslaved more cruelly than ever before. Around 200 Africans are recorded as having been brutally beaten during this period; the slightest sign of anything but total subservience could be taken as a threat.

After six weeks, Turner and his band were discovered. He and fifty-five others were found to be involved in the rebellion, and they were publicly hanged as an example to all enslaved people that revolting was fruitless. Turner had hoped to set his people free, but instead, his rebellion backfired horribly. Talk of emancipation in the South came to an abrupt halt. Southerners were shocked by the murder of the Travis family; they now feared the people they had enslaved, and they treated them with the kind of brutality that is born of terror. Southerners were more determined to make sure that Africans could never walk free in the South.

This was a huge setback for abolitionists in the South, but their Northern counterparts continued to work tirelessly in a bid to get rid of slavery in their beloved country. In 1831, Garrison founded the New England Anti-Slavery Society. He was not yet thirty years old, but he had already proven himself to be one of America's most passionate abolitionists.

It was unsurprising then that when the American Anti-Slavery Society was formed in 1833, Garrison was among its first leaders. And he would soon be joined by a man who became a lifelong inspiration and friend, not only to Garrison but to abolitionists and enslaved people throughout the United States: the now-famous Frederick Douglass.

The Escape of Frederick Douglass

After Nat Turner's rebellion, Southerners began treating their own enslaved people with more cruelty than ever before. In addition, the laws surrounding slavery were made more restrictive and were enforced more diligently. One of these regulations regarded the education of Africans. Plantation owners quickly latched onto the fact that Turner was literate, using this information to resist any form of education for enslaved people. In fact, anyone found to be involved with educating Africans could be harshly fined and even imprisoned for several months.

One person who was deeply affected by the laws surrounding education was Frederick Douglass, who was only thirteen years old at the time of the rebellion. Like almost all Africans in the South, Douglass had been born into slavery, sometime in 1818; his exact date of birth is unknown. (The same farmers and plantation owners that kept diligent records of the births and pedigrees of their prized foxtrotting horses did not apply the same respect to their slaves; dates of birth were seldom ever recorded.)

Douglass may have been the son of one of the plantation owners in Talbot County, Maryland. This was not an uncommon occurrence; slave owners considered enslaved women to be their property, and they frequently bore children with them. These children were invariably slaves and were seldom treated any better than other enslaved children, but Douglass was raised in the home of the plantation owner. However, he was still considered a slave.

Nonetheless, the wife of one of the plantation owners, Sophia Auld, took pity on the little boy growing up in her home. In 1830, when Douglass was twelve, she decided that no child growing up in her house would be allowed to go without an education. She started to teach Douglass the alphabet, planning to teach him how to read and write.

Nat Turner's rebellion quickly put a stop to all that. The beginnings of literacy were just starting to open up a new world for Douglass when Sophia Auld's husband, upon hearing what had happened in Virginia, forbade her from teaching Douglass another lesson. Auld didn't dare to contradict her husband. Nonetheless, Douglass had had a taste of literacy, and he refused to give up on it. Neighbors and the white children he grew up with secretly helped him learn to read and write. By the age of sixteen, Douglass was not only literate but also eloquent.

Perhaps sensing that Douglass would cause trouble, his owner decided to hire him out to a fellow plantation owner named William Freeland. Here, Douglass really started to spread his wings for the first time. He was likely the only African person on the entire plantation who was capable of reading and writing. He somehow got his hands on a Bible, and he grew passionate about teaching its message to his fellow enslaved people. Soon he was holding church-like meetings every week. But he wasn't only teaching enslaved people about theology; he was also teaching them how to read, using the New Testament as his textbook.

Surprisingly enough, Freeland was aware of these meetings, but he didn't seem to mind them. However, he was one of the few who approved of such meetings. Gatherings of Africans without any white people present were completely illegal, and the fact that Douglass could read was a scandal enough in itself. Other plantation owners ambushed one of the gatherings. They stoned the Africans who had come to drink from the well of knowledge, beating them with clubs and dispersing them. After that, no more gatherings were held.

The damage to Douglass's reputation was great. Douglass was considered to be nothing but a troublemaker, and his owner, who was Thomas Auld at this point, decided to send him to Edward Covey. Covey was a brutal, hard man with a sadistic streak, and he was known as a "slave-breaker." He broke the bodies of enslaved people in a bid to break their spirits, and many enslaved people returned from a stint with him with all the fight taken out of them.

Douglass was soon given plenty of reason to fear Covey. He was terribly abused and regularly beaten for the tiniest infraction. Douglass soon found his own bright spirit waning. His passion for freedom and knowledge began to dim in the face of the pain inflicted upon him. But one day, as Covey prepared to give Douglass yet another savage beating, something snapped within the young enslaved man. He rose up against Covey and fought him, no longer cowering in the face of the lash, and physically overcame the slave-breaker. Covey was terrified of Douglass and never beat him again.

This experience was an empowering one for Douglass, who realized that he didn't have to lie down and take whatever life threw at him. His body was enslaved, but his heart longed for freedom, and if he could overcome Edward Covey, maybe he could overcome his shackles. It wasn't long before Douglass was planning his escape.

He was assisted by a young woman who had stolen his heart: Anna Murray. She was a freedwoman from nearby Baltimore, and she wanted nothing more than for her treasured beau to be free like she was. In the summer of 1834, Douglass and Murray worked together to plan a way for him to get out of slavery forever. Several attempts were foiled, and fall had come softly to the hills of Maryland by the time Douglass made his final bid for freedom.

Murray provided him with identification documents, and on September 3ʳᵈ, Douglass slipped out of Covey's farm for the last time. He boarded a train that took him to New York, his false papers proving good enough to fool anyone who asked for them. It was a long and heart-pounding journey by rail. Even though New York was a free state, Douglass could have easily been dragged back to captivity if someone had known he was a slave.

At last, Douglass found himself walking into the home of a man who actually wanted to set enslaved people free. His name was David Ruggles, and he was an abolitionist and a free African. Ruggles had opened up his home as a safe house for runaway slaves, and Douglass was able to stay there for as long as it took him to find his feet in a free world. He wasted absolutely no time in doing the one thing that he had always wanted. On September 15ᵗʰ, just twelve days after his escape, Douglass married Anna Murray. Now registered as a freedman, Douglass moved to New Bedford, Massachusetts, where he settled with Anna.

Douglass would prove to be a disloyal husband, but he never wavered in his faithfulness to one thing: the cause of abolition. He later became a close ally of William Lloyd Garrison and worked together with the Anti-Slavery Society to abolish slavery. He wrote one of the most hard-hitting eyewitness accounts of slavery ever penned, the *Narrative of the Life of Frederick Douglass*. The book became wildly popular in the North as soon as it was published, not only because of the brutality it showcased in Douglass's own life and the lives of other enslaved people but also because of its eloquence. This book proved to Northerners that Africans were not stupid or inferior after all.

However, the cause closest to Douglass's heart was that of helping other runaway slaves such as himself. He had gotten out of his shackles and made his way to freedom, and now he was living the life he had always dreamed of. He was married to the woman he loved, lived in a house he owned, and wrote and published numerous books. He wanted that for his brethren in bondage as well.

And that would mean that they needed many more fake ID documents. They needed many more trips by train. And they needed many, many more homes like Ruggles's in which to shelter.

In short, they needed to form the Underground Railroad.

Chapter 4 – The Father of the Underground Railroad

Levi Coffin, one of many Quaker abolitionists and Underground Railroad stationmasters.

https://commons.wikimedia.org/wiki/File:Levi_coffin.JPG

By the time Frederick Douglass had made his daring escape, half of America had allowed for Africans to live in freedom, if not in equality, with their white counterparts. However, the so-called "free states" were still not perfect sanctuaries for runaway slaves.

The Need to Escape to Canada

The many Northern states that had already abolished slavery hoped that the 1787 Constitutional Convention would be a golden opportunity for abolition throughout the United States. Several states petitioned for slavery to be abolished. The Southern states were ready for this resistance from the North. They were quick to have the Constitution not only unchanged on the subject of allowing slavery but also added a new clause to the Constitution called the Fugitive Slave Clause. This allowed for slaves escaping to the free states to be captured and returned to their Southern owners.

Matters were only made worse six years later. Under relentless pressure from the wealthy South, Congress passed the Fugitive Slave Act of 1793. This act caused outrage throughout the North and great satisfaction in the South. It was now fully legal for Southern slave owners and bounty hunters (known as slave catchers) to search for escaped slaves in the free states. In fact, the residents of free states were not even allowed to give sanctuary to runaway slaves and could be fined $500 for doing so. This would be the equivalent of over $13,000 today, which shows it was no small matter.

Once slave catchers captured an escapee, they had to appear in court, and the owner of the enslaved person had to prove ownership. But hard proof wasn't even really necessary. The law stipulated that judges would be paid $5 for proving that a suspected slave was actually a free person; however, if the judge ruled that the suspected slave did belong to the slave owner, they would be paid $10. This was only about a $13 difference in today's money, but for many judges, it was worth more than the price of a person's freedom.

Slave catching became a booming business, as bounty hunters traveled to the free states to search for escaped slaves. Enslaved people were not cheap to buy in the South, and it often proved more economical for slave owners to pay slave catchers than to simply buy another enslaved person if one of theirs escaped. Slave catchers stood to earn a lot of money for very little risk. The law couldn't touch them. Even the residents of free states who believed passionately in abolition had no means of standing against them.

Thus, escaping to the free states was not enough. The free states were not truly free. There was no real freedom for escaped slaves within the United States, but Canada was another story.

In the early 19th century, Canada was still a British colony, and by the time Frederick Douglass made his daring escape in 1834, slavery had been abolished throughout the British Empire for a year. If an escaped slave could escape to Canada, there was no way slave catchers could follow them there. The mighty British Empire would not take kindly to having American slave catchers prowling around its territory. This gave fugitive slaves a fighting chance, but only if they could make it there. It was a long, risky trek, as they had to travel thousands of miles through territory that slave catchers constantly prowled.

Despite this, every year since the Fugitive Slave Act was passed, judges tried as many as 5,000 cases of escaped slaves. About 1,000 people escaped successfully from slavery every year. Escape was dangerous, and it often proved to be unsuccessful—that was until the arrival of the Underground Railroad.

"Tell Them I Love Them All"

One of the very first people to assist fugitive slaves on their route to the free states and ultimately Canada was, unsurprisingly, a Quaker.

Isaac T. Hopper's parents were not members of the Society of Friends when he was born in 1771. His father had married a non-Quaker and been disowned, but they would both return to the Society of Friends when Hopper was about twenty years old. He grew up in

New Jersey, and at the age of sixteen, he became an apprentice to a tailor in Philadelphia. It was here that Hopper would become the very first "stationmaster" of the Underground Railroad—long before either term was ever coined.

It didn't take long before Hopper had his own house and business as a tailor in Philadelphia, and over the next four decades, his home would become a haven for around 1,000 escaped slaves. Hopper's heart was deeply moved by the plight of those who suffered in bondage, and he would stop at nothing to seek their freedom. In 1796, twelve years after he first started rescuing escaped slaves, the Pennsylvania Abolition Society made him a member.

Hopper thrived in this role. His goal was simple: to set people free. Since the British Empire had not yet abolished slavery at the time, Canada wasn't any safer for escaped slaves than the Northern United States, and the escapees' only hope was to somehow become freed people. Although Hopper was just a tailor and had received minimal education, he took it upon himself to learn the fugitive slave laws inside and out. Soon he had developed a knack for twisting the law and finding all kinds of tiny legalities that would enable him to argue an African person's freedom in court. Thanks to Hopper, hundreds of escapees were set free and were able to live out their lives in the United States without the fear of returning to bondage.

In 1792, Hopper had become a member of the Religious Society of Friends, returning to the Quaker faith about a year after his parents did the same. This enabled him to marry Sarah Tatum, who was also a Quaker, after a three-year courtship. Sarah proved to be fully on board with Hopper's abolitionist work, and the two of them worked together to turn their home into a sanctuary.

The Hopper house must have been a very chaotic one at times. Sarah gave birth to twelve children, and in addition to the members of the Hopper family, the house was also sheltering an escapee or two most of the time. However, in this madness, many escapees found new beginnings. They found hope, freedom, and the glorious promise of what life in the free world could be like.

Hopper lost his beloved Sarah in 1822; he had also lost four of his children too. A little less than two years later, he married Hannah Attmore. She, too, was helpful in his work to save escaped slaves. The Hopper home would continue to shelter escapees in Philadelphia until 1829.

That year, division struck the Religious Society of Friends. Elias Hicks, a friend of Hopper's, began to teach controversial concepts, which led to a profound divide in the Society. Hopper, of course, was a dedicated Hicksite. He was pressured to leave Philadelphia entirely, and he packed up his vast family (Hannah had given him four children too) and moved to New York City to run a bookstore.

Hopper was by no means inactive when it came to abolition. This was evident in 1834 when an angry crowd of anti-abolitionists attacked the store, threatening to kill Hopper. This failed to deter him from his abolitionist activities. Four years later, Hopper was still sheltering escapees, and he was assisted by David Ruggles—the same man who had helped Frederick Douglass to escape.

Hopper and Ruggles were all too happy to help when a new escapee named Thomas Hughes showed up at Hopper's door. Hopper provided him with sustenance and shelter, but a few days later, he was horrified to discover that the man he was protecting was not just a fugitive slave but also a thief. He had stolen $8,000 from his owner in the process of his escape—a tremendous sum that equates to around half a million dollars in today's money. Ruggles and Hopper were faced with a difficult decision when it came to Hughes's future. As always, Hopper's keen sense of justice won out. He contacted Hughes's owner and offered to pay back the majority of the sum but only if the owner would set Hughes free. Faced with losing that kind of money, the owner was only too happy to agree. Hughes served time in prison for his crime, but when he walked out of prison, he did it as a freedman.

By 1840, the American Anti-Slavery Society led by William Lloyd Garrison was gaining strength and support. Joined by Frederick Douglass and others, Garrison was fighting hard for African freedom. He offered Hopper a position within the Society, and Hopper, of course, was all too happy to accept. Despite his age—he was nearly seventy—Hopper would serve faithfully for five years as the treasurer of the Society.

In 1845, Hopper resigned. He had done more for the abolitionist cause than almost anyone else by that time. Still, his philanthropic work was not finished yet. He would spend the rest of his life working with prison inmates before his peaceful death in 1852. His last words seemed to characterize his life, controversial though it often was: "Tell them I love them all."

Levi Coffin

Another influential Quaker who helped enslaved people escape was Levi Coffin. He became one of the earliest "stationmasters" of what was to become known as the Underground Railroad.

Coffin was born into a profoundly Quaker family in New Garden, North Carolina, on October 28th, 1789. He grew up surrounded by slavery, yet like all Quakers in that time (thanks to the efforts of Benjamin Lay), he was an abolitionist. Coffin grew up as an uneducated farm boy. However, he didn't need an education to see slavery for what it truly was, a brutal and barbaric institution. He hated the injustice of it, and his heart went out to the enslaved people he saw all around him.

Coffin didn't have an easy youth. Working and living on the farm was hard, and his parents were uninterested in providing him with an education, even though Coffin was determined to become a teacher someday. Unlike his enslaved counterparts, Coffin was able to pursue an education on his own terms. He became a teacher around 1821 when he was in his thirties, and his first move was an unconventional and borderline illegal one: he opened a school specifically for enslaved people.

While enslaved people couldn't attend a regular school or daily classes, Coffin managed to find a loophole by opening a Sunday school, teaching religion as well as literacy. North Carolina was fairly liberal for a slave state, and many slave owners allowed their slaves to attend. Those who opposed the idea were not content with simply keeping their enslaved people from attending. They began to protest the school with violence, and soon, this hatred spread to include the entire Quaker community.

Coffin was forced to abandon his beloved Sunday school just five years after opening it. He and his family, along with many other Quakers, moved to Indiana to avoid the growing resentment of slave owners. Indiana was a free state, but Coffin found work there to help further the cause of enslaved people. He had two great passions: helping escapees and proving to the world that slavery was an institution that the economy could survive without.

In Indiana, Coffin started what he called a "free produce" store. He sold only goods that had been produced without the use of any enslaved people. The idea was successful, if unpopular, and Coffin was able to turn a profit. At the same time, he also became a part of the Underground Railroad, which was in its infancy, opening up his home as a depot for runaways.

Coffin's far-thinking approach extended even beyond the days of the Underground Railroad. During the American Civil War, he worked to ensure that ex-slaves were provided with an education and were integrated into free society. Coffin continued to work tirelessly well into his old age. He retired in 1869, after suffrage had been granted to African Americans, when he was eighty years old.

William Still

Isaac T. Hopper had done excellent work when it came to sheltering escapees and helping them to find a new life in the United

States and beyond. However, he was working almost in isolation. The Underground Railroad itself, as an extensive network of safe houses, would be formed later by a free African American named William Still.

Even though Still was born a free man under New Jersey law, slavery was still something that was very close to his childhood, something that was instrumental in making him into an abolitionist hero. His father, Levin Still, was born into slavery and had to pay for his freedom. His mother had a far more tragic story. Born in Maryland as a slave, Charity—previously called Sidney—had married Levin while enslaved, but she never had the opportunity to buy her freedom. Since their marriage was not considered legally binding, Levin moved to New Jersey alone, leaving his wife and four children behind in Maryland.

Charity's only recourse was to escape, and she did so, taking her two boys and two little girls with her. The little family had a joyous taste of freedom, but it was a short-lived one. Slave catchers caught up to Charity and the children, and since the children legally belonged to Charity's owner (not to the man who had fathered them), they and their mother were all forced to return to slavery. Charity was dragged from a nice little New Jersey farm back to some hovel on a Maryland plantation, to beatings and chastisement, to separation from her treasured children.

She couldn't stay there. Somehow, she escaped again. However, this time, she was unable to bring her two sons, Levin Jr. and Peter, with her. They remained in slavery, while Charity took her two little girls and fled back to New Jersey and to Levin's arms.

This time, Charity's freedom would be permanent, although she was still technically a slave under federal law. She and Levin settled on their farm in New Jersey, and she tried her best not to think of the two children she had left behind in Maryland. She gave birth to an astounding fourteen more children. The youngest was a little boy, born on October 7th, 1821. (Unlike Frederick Douglass, who was born three years earlier, this child would grow up with a birthday.) She named him William, and he grew up knowing freedom, but with the echoes of his parents' stories of slavery ringing in his ears. Horrifically, William was legally a slave under the Fugitive Slave Act. Although he would never experience slavery, federal law deemed him to be the property of the man who had owned Charity.

William Still grew up knowing that the gift of freedom he experienced every day, the gift of literacy and of being able to have some control over his own fate, was one that many of his fellows—even some of his own family—would never have. This knowledge, perhaps, made him restless. Still didn't stay in New Jersey for long. In 1844, at the age of twenty-three, he moved to Philadelphia.

It was a fateful moment. Philadelphia was then still very much a Quaker town, and the Quakers had been abolitionists for seventy years by the time Still got there. Its proximity to the Maryland border and its abolitionist nature made the city a refuge for many fleeing enslaved persons. Isaac T. Hopper had also left behind a legacy of sheltering escapees in the homes of abolitionists. Still had barely arrived in Philadelphia when he, too, was inspired by this cause.

Three years after his arrival in Philadelphia, Still's fate as an active abolitionist was sealed when he was employed as a clerk by the Pennsylvania Anti-Slavery Society, or PASS. It was also in 1847 that he married and settled into a home. Still would shelter numerous slaves here, including the wife of John Brown, the ex-slave who famously raided Harper's Ferry (with Still's help).

But unlike Hopper, Still would not become famous for the many escapees he helped from his own home. Still created more than a single refuge—he created an entire network of them.

It had become obvious to the members of PASS that something had to be done to help the fleeing escapees get through Pennsylvania and the other free states and reach the hallowed ground of Canada. To this end, a new committee was formed: the Philadelphia Vigilance

Committee. Its founder, Robert Purvis, was a man of mixed race whose father had been an early abolitionist. Robert had started the Vigilance Committee in 1838, and it was revived now out of sheer necessity. These people would watch out for escapees and squirrel them away in safe houses, arranging everything that was necessary to get them out of the United States. In 1850, the Vigilance Committee was made more necessary than ever.

With tensions rising between the North and South, and secession looking more and more inevitable, Senator Henry Clay attempted to bring peace to the nation with the Compromise of 1850. It was less of a compromise than it was a kowtow to the South, one that would enrage Northerners and maintain only eleven years of tenuous peace. In it, a new law was passed that not only forbade free citizens from assisting escapees but also forced them to assist slave catchers in capturing them. Huge fines and significant jail time would be the penalty for anyone who dared to help an escaped slave. One Massachusetts abolitionist, Jonathan Walker, faced an even more humiliating and painful punishment. He was a captain at sea and attempted to help enslaved people escape via ship. He was caught and punished not only with fines and imprisonment but also by having a hot iron applied to his hand, branding the letters SS into his skin. The initials stood for "Slave Stealer."

Of course, this was no reason for PASS to back down. Instead, its Vigilance Committee became more active than ever. Still was its leader and mastermind, and together with other abolitionists— including many African Americans, as well as white Americans, such as Passmore Williamson—they would successfully help hundreds of escapees get through Pennsylvania and into Canada. Still documented helping around 800 of them personally.

One of the escapees Still met was a man named Peter, who was several years older than Still. Peter had the wild-eyed, desperate look of a man who had been enslaved for forty years. He had somehow managed to escape his Alabama owner and find his way to the comparative haven of Philadelphia. Peter, at least, had no need to escape to Canada; he had been able to purchase his freedom. He stayed in Philadelphia and turned his attention to two missions: first, to free his wife and three children, and second, to find his parents.

Still kept meticulous records of the escapees who passed through Philadelphia, interviewing them all, and Peter went to him in an attempt to find his parents, telling Still that they had both once been slaves as well. Peter's father had been able to buy his freedom, but his mother was forced to escape twice, once with Peter and the second time leaving him behind. The story sounded all too familiar. Still asked the names of Peter's parents, and he told him that they were Levin and Sidney.

Still was dumbstruck. He had just met his older brother, one of the two boys who his mother had no choice but to leave behind in Maryland when she escaped for the second time. There was a tearful reunion, which grew more tearful when Still asked what happened to Levin Jr., his other older brother. Peter's news was deeply tragic. Levin Jr. had been brutally murdered by an overseer, who had whipped him to death. This appalling, gruesome killing would have earned the man a death penalty if his victim had been white, but because Levin Jr. was a slave, his murderer would continue to walk free.

The knowledge that one of his own blood had perished as a slave pushed Still to continue rescuing as many escapees as he could. His system of safe houses grew, and his cunning in hiding escapees continued to thwart the many efforts of slave catchers seeking to capture these fleeing refugees. Of course, not all of Still's attempts were successful. The Compromise of 1850 had made it almost impossible for escapees to go free if they were caught. And they also made life dangerous for the courageous abolitionists who helped them, as Still would find out in the case of Jane Johnson.

The Rescue of Jane Johnson

When Jane Johnson heard that her owner, Colonel John Wheeler, was traveling through Pennsylvania, she knew this could be her one chance for a better life, and not only for herself but also for her two little sons, Daniel and Isaiah.

Johnson had been born into slavery and had spent the past two years of her life in service to the colonel. She'd been purchased at an auction along with her two younger boys; her older son had been torn from her arms and sold to another buyer, never to be seen again. The experience was enough to crush any mother. For enslaved women, though, it was a reality of life.

But with the news of Wheeler's travels, Johnson realized that slavery might not have to be her reality forever. While the Fugitive Slave Act rendered any escaped slave who traveled to a free state to still be legally the property of their owner, if the owner willingly brought an enslaved person into Pennsylvania, that person was legally considered to be free. Knowing this, when Johnson was told to prepare for travel, she told Wheeler that she was bringing her two little boys with her. For whatever reason, Wheeler agreed, although it is unknown why Wheeler was so adamant about bringing Jane with him on his journey in the first place.

As much as Wheeler appeared to be reasonable when it came to letting Johnson's two sons travel with them, that was where his kindness ended. Wheeler had been cautioned against coming to Pennsylvania lest he lose his valuable property, but he had absolutely no intentions of giving up what he considered to be rightfully his. In his arrogance, he believed the law wouldn't apply to him. Besides, he would only spend a few days in Pennsylvania before heading on his way to New York. He didn't think Johnson would try anything.

He was wrong. On July 18th, 1855, as soon as he settled down for a luxurious dinner at Bloodgood's Hotel in Philadelphia, Johnson saw her chance. Many of the servers in the restaurant, where she sat apart from her owner, were free African Americans. She had seen many Africans performing menial tasks like these before; the difference was that here, these people were getting paid, and they could go home to their families when the day's work was done. Desperately, she caught the attention of one of the African servers and told him that she was enslaved but that she wanted to be free.

The man quickly took action. He hastily contacted the Philadelphia Vigilance Committee, and William Still and several of his allies leaped into action. Johnson waited in suspense as Still planned a way to get her from Wheeler. She was legally free here, but getting her away from her master was no simple matter; Wheeler could turn violent, and while the law was on Johnson's side, the local judge definitely wouldn't be. He had been ruling against African Americans time and time again. The only safe way to get Johnson and her sons to freedom was to snatch her away from Wheeler and get her into hiding as quickly as possible.

And they had to act quickly. When Still received the message, Johnson and Wheeler were only half an hour away from boarding the boat that would take them to New York and beyond the reach of the Vigilance Committee. Their only hope at freedom was to escape the steamboat itself, and this was exactly where Still planned to stage his daring rescue.

Enlisting the aid of another Vigilance Committee member, Passmore Williamson (who was useful for both his determination and his pale skin; people didn't ask questions of why Africans were traveling with him), Still headed for the wharf where Johnson and her sons were waiting aboard the steamboat. He spotted the young woman and her two boys on deck and approached. Unfortunately, Wheeler had also joined them, and Still boldly strode into his presence.

Pennsylvania was free of slavery, but it was by no means free of racism. To approach and confront a white man was almost unthinkable for most African Americans, let alone a slave owner from the South itself. But Still did it fearlessly. After all, it had become his life's work.

He addressed Johnson first, asking if she was traveling with someone. She indicated Wheeler, and Still fell silent, allowing Passmore Williamson to do the talking to Wheeler. Williamson turned to the colonel, telling him that he wanted to tell his "servant," which was a direct insult to Wheeler, as he considered Johnson to be his slave, about her rights. Wheeler scoffed. In his eyes, Jane Johnson had no more rights than a horse or a cow. He told Williamson scathingly that she knew her rights.

Unluckily for the arrogant Wheeler, Johnson knew her rights, and she knew that freedom was within her grasp if these two gentlemen—a black and a white man, who were working together on equal footing—would help her take it. She clutched her crying boys and told Still and Williamson that she wanted to be free.

"You are as free as your master," said Williamson.

Despite cries of outrage from the crowd, who demanded to know why Wheeler's "property" was being taken from him, Williamson grabbed Johnson's hand. Wheeler was outraged. He assaulted Williamson, but it was too late. Still and a few helpful bystanders grabbed Johnson and the boys and hightailed it off the steamboat and into the streets. Williamson and Wheeler were still engaged in a scuffle when Still reached his waiting horse and carriage. He bundled Johnson and the children into it while Wheeler shouted angrily for a nearby policeman to seize Still and the fleeing Johnsons. Mercifully, the policeman declined, and the carriage galloped off into the streets, spiriting Johnson and her children off to safety.

That was the last day Jane, Daniel, and Isaiah Johnson ever spent in slavery. Still smuggled them all into hiding, and they were able to live out their days as free citizens of the United States. Still, however, was nearly denied this privilege himself. The outraged Wheeler turned to the corrupt local judge and opened a court case against Still,

Williamson, and the dock workers who had helped to get the Johnsons to freedom. Still managed to avoid imprisonment, but Williamson spent several weeks behind bars as a hot legal battle was fought. (Frederick Douglass was one of Williamson's many visitors as he waited for the verdict.) While Pennsylvania law viewed the Johnsons as free people, federal law declared them slaves, and the high-profile court case became a hard-fought battle.

Williamson may well have been left with a heavy prison sentence, and his career as an abolitionist and hero may have come to an end if it wasn't for Johnson herself. She came out of hiding to play savior to her savior, witnessing in court that she had decided to go free of her own accord. She stated that Williamson had neither stolen her, nor caused a riot, nor assaulted her former master. Her rousing testimony was made at terrible personal risk, and Pennsylvanian officials and the Vigilance Committee had to smuggle her back out of Philadelphia with great caution. Ultimately, though, it paid off. Still and Williamson were not charged with any crimes, and they were able to continue their work with saving people who had escaped from slavery.

The Underground Railroad

From the revival of the Vigilance Committee in 1850 until the American Civil War's end in 1865, William Still would smuggle hundreds of slaves to safety, but he was certainly not alone the way Isaac Hopper had been. Instead, he established a vast network of safe houses and sympathizers, which stretched all the way from the Canadian border through the Northern United States and even into the South itself. This clandestine operation kept almost no records; most of what we know comes from Still himself. He personally interviewed many of the escapees he helped and kept records of them in an attempt to keep families together. These would all later be published in his book, *The Underground Railroad Records*, in 1872.

The "Underground Railroad" was the name that he and other abolitionists gave to the network of safe houses that helped thousands of slaves cross into Canada. It wasn't really underground, although underground trails would be invented decades later. And while it didn't involve a physical railroad, it used railroad terminology simply because that was the most common mode of transportation at the time. Safe houses were called "depots," and the people who lived in them were known as "stationmasters." There were also "conductors" who helped move enslaved people across miles of hostile territory, sometimes by real trains but also on foot or by road.

"Agents" were some of the bravest of the lot. These courageous men and women lived in the South or on the very border of it, and they would be the first people that escapees contacted. They would help the escapees get on the Railroad. Some of them even actively sought out enslaved people to help; they might even pose as slaves themselves, hiding out in slave owners' homes or plantations in order to give hope and direction to enslaved people. Of course, along with their enslaved brethren, these "agents" would suffer the same atrocities that they did.

There were even Underground Railroad members in Canada itself, and they helped escapees to find their feet in a free country. While Canada was by no means free of racism, and equality was still a long way in the future, at least African people could live their own lives and make their own choices.

The escapees themselves were often called "cargo." While this may seem like a dehumanizing label for people who had been treated like objects their entire lives, there was a good reason for this. The Underground Railroad's messages were all encoded. People would be called "hams" or other objects that were often transported, which helped to prevent arousing suspicion.

William Still is known as the "Father of the Underground Railroad," and he remained its leader and coordinator throughout its existence. However, he was by no means the only hero of the Underground Railroad. Many of the Railroad's members were free Africans, like him, or abolitionist whites, like Williamson.

And some of them had known the bitter taste of slavery themselves. None were more famous than arguably the Railroad's greatest conductor, Harriet Tubman.

Chapter 5 – The Moses of Her People

This photograph of Harriet Tubman captures the remarkable expression in her steely eyes.

https://commons.wikimedia.org/wiki/File:Tubman,_Harriet_Ross.jpg

While untold hundreds of people worked as conductors on the Underground Railroad, the one whose story is most well known and provides the most vivid glimpse into the traveling conditions on the Railroad is Harriet Tubman. Her past was a brutal one, and despite the fact that she was an enslaved African woman—then considered to be at the very bottom of the social pecking order—she would become one of the most remarkable figures in abolitionist history.

I'll Split His Head Open!

Harriet Tubman, born Araminta Ross around 1820 in Dorchester County, Maryland, was one of very few slaves who learned in childhood that resistance was possible.

Young Minty's grandmother had been born free. Minty knew her as Modesty Green from her mother's stories, but long Modesty once had an African name and had walked across the wilds of her native continent as a free person. She came across the barbaric Middle Passage, as so many others did, and became a slave. Her daughter, Harriet "Rit" Green, would become a cook in the home of a wealthy woman named Mary Brodess.

When Mary Brodess married Anthony Thompson, young Rit met the love of her life: Ben Ross. Ben, like Rit, was an enslaved person working on Thompson's plantation. Their marriage meant nothing in the eyes of their owners, but it was certainly a fertile one. Rit wanted nothing more than a family, and she bore one child after the other, even though she was bringing them into a world filled with uncertainty and suffering. Perhaps she had hope that someday her children would grow up in a better world. Little did she know that one of her children would be instrumental in bringing that hope to the nation.

Of course, Rit didn't know that she'd given birth to one of the Underground Railroad's most famous heroes. However, she did know that she wanted to keep her little family together at whatever cost. For an enslaved woman, this was a fruitless quest. It was hard enough to simply carry a child to term and bring a healthy baby into the world.

There was no such thing as maternity leave for enslaved people—there was no such thing as leave at all. Rit would have continued to perform her duties as a cook right up until each child was born. She would nurse and care for her baby in between working, and she would possibly face severe physical punishment if she ever valued the child over the family that she unwillingly served. Then there was the matter of raising a child. Many slave owners provided no healthcare and utterly minimal food to the people they had enslaved. While keeping her children alive was a monumental challenge, it was one that the ever-determined Rit tackled with unending tenacity.

Despite all this, Rit would inevitably be separated from her children. Slave owners encouraged the people they enslaved to reproduce, not so they could experience the joy of parenthood, but so their children could be sold or rented out for a fee. They profited from children that were little more than toddlers, dragging four- and five-year-old children from the arms of their mothers and into a brutal workforce. Rit's children were no exception. Minty had three older sisters she would never meet. Soph, Linah, and Mariah Ritty would all be sold off to a different owner before she was even born. Rit never saw her cherished daughters, the babies she had fought so hard for, again.

Still, Minty was able to experience her toddler years with some other siblings. Rit had nine children in total. Minty knew five of them: her older brother Robert, her younger sister Rachel, and her three younger brothers, Ben, Henry, and Moses. Ben and Henry would remain in the employ of the Brodess family for the rest of their lives. Moses, however, was not needed on the plantation, and he was a strong little child with a promising future as a useful enslaved person. A Georgian trader quickly noticed the little boy, and he met with Edward Brodess, Mary Brodess's son, who inherited the slaves after her death in 1810, as he was interested in purchasing him.

The moment Rit got wind of the offer, she was incensed. She had already lost three children. Every night, she had to lie awake thinking about those three little girls, about all the awful things that a young enslaved girl could suffer. She wasn't about to relinquish Moses without a fight. She hid him away with the help of some of the other enslaved people and succeeded in concealing him from Brodess for several weeks.

But Rit couldn't hide Moses forever. Her next course of action was to do the unthinkable. She spoke to Edward Brodess about the sale, demanding that Brodess cancel the transaction. Brodess was furious. He couldn't believe that a mere enslaved woman like Rit would confront him in that manner, and he decided he was done playing cat and mouse with the errant Rit. He was going to bring the slave trader right into Rit's quarters and drag the child away, kicking and screaming.

Rit grew desperate. As the trader and Brodess approached the door of the hovel that Rit and her children called home, the courageous enslaved woman stood in the doorway, ready to do battle. She was just one woman, and she had no real weapons, but she was a lioness ready to fight to the very death if need be. "The first man that comes into my house, I will split his head open!" she cried.

The threat may have seemed ludicrous coming from a lone woman faced with an angry slave trader. Edward Brodess, however, saw something fierce and indomitable in Rit's eyes, something that refused to back down. Brodess knew better than to get between a lioness and her cubs, and he decided not to sell Moses after all.

Minty was likely not living with her mother anymore at the time of Moses's prospective sale, but the story became a legend among the plantation slaves. Minty would likely have heard the story over and over—in suitable tones of respect and awe—from her two other brothers, Ben and Henry, who remained close to her for much of her enslaved life. It was something that deeply affected Minty, as it showed her that fighting back was a possibility. It was also something she most likely didn't witness with her own eyes, for when Minty was only five years old, she, too, was torn from her mother's arms.

A Five-Year-Old Nursemaid

Ever since she was a little girl, young Minty had been caring for her younger siblings. As much as slave owners wanted their slaves to reproduce, they by no means wished for enslaved women to shirk any of their duties in favor of caring for their children. Rit had no choice but to leave her babies behind in the slave quarters. The only people available there to care for those children were children themselves, those too young to contribute any meaningful effort in the eyes of the slave owners. Minty was only a toddler when she was left to care for her baby siblings.

When Mary Brodess, Rit's owner, died in 1810, she left her plantation and enslaved people to her son, Edward. He was too young to take legal ownership of the plantation at the time, so in the meantime, they were under the care of Ben's owner, Anthony Thompson. When Minty was around four years old, Edward came of age. He took over the plantation, and life immediately became harder for Minty.

By the time Minty was about five, she already had years of experience nursing Rachel, Ben, Henry, and possibly even infant Moses. She was still little more than a baby herself, but it didn't take Edward Brodess long to realize that Minty was good at caring for babies. This made her valuable, and she was a commodity in Brodess's eyes. Rit was appalled to have poor little Minty taken from her, and the little child could hardly have been expected to understand why she was being taken away from the only home she'd ever known. All Minty knew was that she was being sent away to live among strangers.

Minty's new role was, at least, one that would feel somewhat familiar to her. She was given the care of a slave owner's newborn baby, or rather, part of the care of the baby. Her job was a simple one in her renter's eyes: she had to sit by the slumbering baby's cradle, and if the little one woke up and cried, she had to rock the cradle until it fell asleep again.

It didn't seem to occur to the baby's parents that crying was a normal part of being a baby. Instead, anytime the little baby's piercing shrieks shattered the peace and quiet of its parents' home, Minty was immediately blamed. Her life became a simple and brutal reality. If the baby cried, Minty was whipped. And no matter how much she rocked the cradle or crooned to the baby, there was no way to keep it from crying every single time. She would be beaten every day, often multiple times a day, sometimes many times even before breakfast. And these beatings were no small matter; they left scars on young Minty's skin.

This hardship would have been enough to break the spirit of any five-year-old girl. But it failed to break the spirit of Araminta Ross. Instead, Minty started to find ways to resist, just as her courageous mother had resisted the sale of little Moses. She started to fight back when she was beaten, to wear layers and layers of clothing even in the humid summer to temper the beatings, and even ran away on one occasion. Rebellion bloomed deep in Minty's heart, and it was a blossom that would come to bear great fruit later in her life.

First, though, Minty had to survive her brutal childhood. After her stint as a nursemaid, she was hired out to do far more physical work. At the age of seven, she found herself working outside in the plantation fields, once again living among people she didn't know. Homesickness was the one constant in her young life. At an age when free American children were starting to learn the alphabet, little Minty was carrying heavy traps across the plantations, setting the brutal, sharp-toothed objects to capture the muskrats that posed a threat to plantation owners' crops. It was dangerous work, and it was by no means suitable for a seven-year-old child. The physical hardship started to take its toll on the little girl, and she contracted measles. Of course, this was no reason for the slave owners to give her some time off. Minty continued to work until she could barely stand, and when she was well and truly useless for work, the owners finally sent her back to Brodess's slave quarters. Although she was on the brink of death, Minty was at least reunited with her mother. Rit's efforts managed to keep her alive. Minty recovered but was then torn away from her family yet again to work in the fields.

Minty would later say that she hated working in the house even more than working in the fields. However, the fields were a brutal enough place to grow up. Enslaved people were required to work for as long as there were daylight hours, sometimes as many as eighteen or twenty hours a day, regardless of the weather. Minty was forced to labor for her every waking moment, her tiny limbs toiling under the burning sun, in the freezing cold, or in the pouring rain. Her little hands grew calloused from picking and planting. Her back ached.

But her spirit, her young spirit that had faced so much hardship in its short life, never broke.

"It Broke My Skull"

By the age of twelve, Minty had returned to the Brodess plantation, where she worked alongside her two younger brothers in the fields. Despite the gender roles in the society of the plantation owners, with women treated like delicate creatures to be kept safely inside and suitably married off when the time came, enslaved people worked shoulder to shoulder whether they were men, women, or children. Minty chopped wood, drove a team of oxen, and bent her back over the crops in the fields just like Ben and Henry did.

Of course, this wasn't the only work she did. Her owner could send her anywhere he pleased. When Brodess needed someone to run to the general store in the nearby town, Minty had to go, whether she liked it or not.

Perhaps she enjoyed the change of scenery as she made the journey over to the store and headed up to the counter. The storekeeper was weighing out goods for the customers, using the old method of scales and weights. Those heavy little lead objects were set out on the counter, ready to be used. Minty didn't give them a second glance as she approached the counter. Little did she know that one of them would change her life forever.

Instead, her attention was focused on the African man standing nearby, his expression shifty, his eyes nervous. Minty struck up a conversation with him and discovered that he was a fugitive, perhaps the first escaped slave that she ever met. He'd slipped away from his plantation, and he was looking for the one thing that all enslaved people dreamed of: a way out. A way to freedom.

Minty was still talking with the fugitive in agonized whispers when the door of the general store burst open, and a white man strode in, a man with a whip in his hands and brutality in his eyes. Minty knew who he was all too well. He was an overseer, and like this escapee, she bore the scars of their lashes. The overseer turned to Minty, shouting at her to help him corner the escapee.

Minty, of course, would do no such thing. She refused to help him catch this poor man, and the escapee began to flee. Blind with fury, the overseer reached over to the counter and grabbed a two-pound lead weight, a heavy little object that weighed nothing in his strong hands. Minty saw him raise his hand and aim at the head of the fleeing fugitive, and she stepped forward. The weight struck her instead, smashing into her temple with a force that knocked her to the floor, unconscious.

Later, Minty would say that the terrible impact had broken her skull. This was the only diagnosis her condition was ever afforded, for this twelve-year-old enslaved girl, knocked out cold and bleeding profusely, was given absolutely no medical attention. They might never even have picked her up off the floor and taken her back to the plantation if she hadn't been in the way. She was laid on the seat of a loom and left there to live or die of her own accord.

For two long days, Minty lay, deeply comatose, on the hard surface, blood drying in her hair. Her condition was critical, but no one cared. If she died, she died. Enslaved people could always be replaced. This appalling reality left her alone and suffering.

But she didn't die. Minty woke two days later, and as soon as she was on her feet, she was sent back into the fields, still dizzy from her head injury. It's uncertain whether her skull really did break, but the injury was definitely a severe one, and it would affect her for the rest of her life. Minty would suffer crippling migraines and strange fits of somnolence—something that could have been narcolepsy, hypersomnia, or even cataplexy.

Becoming Harriet Tubman

Minty's worth in the eyes of slave owners instantly decreased the moment that lead weight struck her. She went back to her work as well as she could, but it was nearly impossible. Her headaches were so bad that she could barely see or stay upright; no amount of shouting or threats of punishment could make them go away, no matter how hard Minty tried to work through them.

To make matters worse, her narcolepsy would strike at apparently random moments. Minty would be calmly working in the fields or performing some other duty when she would simply collapse. To all appearances, she fell asleep on her feet. Outraged overseers would whip her prone, unresponsive body in an attempt to make her go back to work, but Minty was deeply unconscious. She couldn't feel anything. Not during the whipping, anyway. When she awoke with her limbs and back covered in throbbing welts, she felt the sting of the sheer awful injustice of it all, almost more keenly than the physical agony.

Edward Brodess may well have sold Minty just to be rid of the nuisance of a half-functional slave if it wasn't for the fact that nobody wanted her. In the eyes of slave buyers, Minty was worse than useless. She continued to work as well as she could on the Brodess plantation, but now she lived in fear of being sold to some buyer desperate enough to spend a few pennies on a woman who could barely work.

Like her mother Rit, Minty was terrified of being separated from her family, and the knowledge that her sale could take place at any moment hung over her head through her every waking minute.

Somehow, though, Minty managed to stay with her family for the next eight years. She worked closely alongside Ben and Henry, who became her best friends. They suffered together, forming a bond that ran deeper even than their familial ties.

While marriages between enslaved people were not legally recognized, this didn't stop enslaved people from marrying—and it didn't stop Minty either. She met John Tubman, a free African American, when he came to the plantation to do some work as a temporary employee. John was quickly taken with the quick-witted Minty despite her health issues. In 1844, when Minty was around twenty-four years old, they married. Unfortunately, their marriage was an unhappy one. Minty may have married John in an attempt to escape slavery since, as a freeman, John could have earned enough money to buy his wife and set her free. This, sadly, never transpired. In fact, John was resistant to Minty's desire to be free.

Perhaps because of this, Minty and John never had children. Minty knew that her babies would be the legal possessions of Edward Brodess and that he could sell them right out of her arms just as many of her own siblings had been sold. She did take John's name when they married and changed her first name to honor her mother. Araminta Ross became Harriet Tubman, a name that would echo through the annals of history.

Escape

Between her unhappy marriage with John and her increasing physical suffering, which heightened her worries about being sold, life in bondage was growing more and more unbearable for Harriet.

The last straw came in 1849. Harriet fell intensely ill, possibly with the headaches that had plagued her since her injury, and her owner decided that he had had enough of this troublesome slave. He started advertising her for sale and entertaining strings of buyers who came to look at her like she was a lame filly up for sale. Harriet's life became a constant flow of humiliation and fear. She knew that each person that looked at her could, at any moment, whisk her away from her husband and family. One by one, they turned her down, disgusted by her physical disability. The stress of it all began to wear on Harriet when another devastating blow struck.

Edward Brodess, who had been Harriet's owner all her life, died. His widow was left with the estate, and she wasn't interested in running a plantation on her own. Instead, she started to hire out and sell as many of the slaves as possible, heedless of the terrible impact this would have on the lives of people who had been together for decades.

Harriet, Ben, and Henry had already been hired out to the son of their father's owner. When they got wind of what was happening on the Brodess plantation, they knew their fates were about to change in terrible ways. Life on the Brodess plantation wasn't easy by any means, but at least it was predictable, and at least they were together. Harriet knew that she would be one of the first to be gotten rid of. She was worth nothing, after all. Brodess's widow would want nothing to do with her.

Desperate, Harriet turned to John, who was absolutely unhelpful. It seemed to matter little to him if his wife was sold right out of his arms. He refused to take action to help her, so Harriet turned to the two people who had been her most trusted confidantes since she was a little girl: Ben and Henry. They, too, were terrified of what was going to happen now that their owner had died. They had wives and families of their own, and they wanted to find some way to keep them together. Harriet convinced them that the only way to keep their families together was to be separated from them for a while. She told them that they needed to leave their wives and children behind and escape to the free world, where they would earn enough money to buy their families back.

This plan seemed like the only way. Even though Ben had an infant baby, he and his brother scraped up the courage to do as their older sister planned. In the depths of the cold night of September 17th, 1849, the three siblings slipped out of the Thompson plantation and headed north.

The plan was short-lived. Even though it took their owner, the widowed Eliza Brodess, more than a week to hear from Thompson that they were gone, Harriet, Ben, and Henry soon began to hear about the bounties that had been placed on their heads. Harriet had been worthless to Brodess when she was still enslaved; however, now that she'd escaped, the woman was willing to pay $100 (the equivalent of about $3,000 today) in order to get her back. This reflected the general attitude of slave owners toward fugitive slaves. The economic impact of fugitive slaves was almost insignificant, but slave owners hated the idea of their valuable property getting up and walking away, and they were willing to go to any lengths to get them back.

Harriet was determined that no bounty should stop them, but this news quickly cowed Ben and Henry. Ben started thinking about what was happening to his wife and baby back on the plantation. Both of them feared their fates if they were found by slave catchers. It was ninety miles to the border of the free world, after all. How could they possibly escape without being noticed?

Harriet encouraged them to keep going, but the young men were adamant. They were going back of their own accord, hopefully to face a lesser punishment than if they were caught. There was no stopping them. Harriet, disgusted, had little choice but to go back with them and face the beating that doubtless awaited them once they returned to the plantation.

But she wouldn't remain at the plantation for long. Harriet had been betrayed by her husband and brothers, the three men who were meant to be on her side, but she was not about to betray her own ideals of freedom.

During the American Revolution, politician Patrick Henry cried, "Give me liberty or give me death!" Now, white Americans like him had their freedom, yet their African counterparts remained in bondage. Harriet echoed his sentiment much later as she faced being sold and separated from her family. She said that she had a right to one of two things, "liberty or death." Life in slavery was no longer an option for her.

So, she escaped again, this time facing the ninety-mile trek alone, with slave catchers stalking her around every corner, with winter coming quickly across the landscape, with no food, no company, and no sure knowledge of which way she should go. She followed the rivers that she knew ran north, and she traveled at night, her eyes fixed upon the North Star.

It's unclear today exactly what route Harriet followed. Because it was well-used at the time by escapees, she kept it secret. However, Preston was probably her first stop. This small community in Maryland was populated by Quakers, and some of them were agents for the Underground Railroad. William Still had not yet developed the Railroad into the nationwide network that it would become, but in a small way, it already existed, as abolitionists used word of mouth to move escapees to homes in Philadelphia, like those of Isaac Hopper.

Harriet made her way to Preston, where the Quakers were quick to help her. They guided her to her next "depot." Leg by agonizing leg, Harriet made her way on foot across Maryland, making treacherous treks between the homes of those who believed all people should be free. Occasionally, "stationmasters" would give her a ride in a cart or wagon to the next depot, but very often, Harriet faced her journey to the next safe house alone and on foot. She traveled by night to avoid slave catchers. It was cold and very dark, and she carried very little provisions with her.

All sorts of methods were employed by the stationmasters to keep Harriet safe. Often, she would pose as an enslaved person to avoid arousing suspicion; sometimes, she performed small menial tasks for the stationmasters, not because they wanted her to work for them but because the sight of a ragged African person at work was so common as to render her completely invisible. No one looked twice at her when she stood in the front yard of a stationmaster's home in broad daylight if she was busy sweeping it.

Occasionally, the trek from one depot to the other took more than a single night. Sometimes Harriet would have to crouch down among the reeds of a marsh during the day, hiding in the stinking mud. Her headaches and narcolepsy had no respect for the fact that one wrong move could cost her her freedom and possibly her life. Every step she took, she was aware that an attack of unconsciousness could come over, leaving her lying in the road where anyone could find her.

Those long, dark nights were times when Harriet clung more staunchly to her faith than ever before. While Rit had never been able to read (Harriet herself would also never be literate), she had passed on the Bible stories that she knew, and Harriet had a deep and fervent belief. Sometimes it was her only companion on those dark roads and through those reeking swamps.

And somehow, it saw her through. Weeks after leaving the plantation and everyone she loved behind, Harriet crossed the border at last and walked into a state that considered her to be a free person: Pennsylvania. She thought of her Bible stories and felt like an Israelite after decades of Egyptian slavery, setting foot at last in the Promised Land. It was a glorious fall morning when Harriet arrived. Her words on her arrival in Pennsylvania have been much quoted, but they bear repeating over and over for their sheer raw power in conveying the experience of a person walking free for the first time. The very sunlight seemed to have a new quality; even Harriet herself felt like crossing that border had made her into something different.

"I looked at my hands to see if I was the same person," she said later. "There was such a glory over everything [...] I felt like I was in Heaven."

It wasn't Heaven; it was only Pennsylvania. But to a person who had spent her whole life in slavery, it was the same thing.

Returning for Kessiah

Philadelphia, while no utopia, was the one thing Harriet had prayed for it to be: a place of freedom. While she was still legally enslaved under federal law, Harriet was treated as a free person in Philadelphia, and perhaps because of her relatively low value, no slave catcher came after her. Since the Fugitive Slave Act of 1850 hadn't yet been passed, no one was compelled to turn her in. She began to lead a free life and make her own choices—and it was wonderful.

By late 1850, Harriet had settled into her life as a proud freedwoman. She had a job as a housekeeper; the domestic tasks that she had found so abhorrent when she was enslaved were now joyous to her because she was being paid for them in money instead of curses and lashes. Yet there was one thing that niggled at her constantly, and that was the thought of her family. She was living a free life, yet they were still in bondage. While she could work set hours and go home to sleep in a real bed in peace every night, her beloved brothers were curled up on the floor of a hovel.

Harriet couldn't bear it. She constantly searched for news about her family, and when the Fugitive Slave Act of 1850 was passed, it didn't drive her to Canada. She lingered in Philadelphia, aware of the Underground Railroad that was rapidly growing and expanding under William Still's leadership. She remembered what the Railroad had done for her and thought of what it could do for her family.

That December, Harriet finally got news of her family, and it wasn't good. Her niece, Kessiah, the daughter of her older sister Linah, was being sold. Like Harriet, Kessiah had married a freeman, but John Bowley wasn't sure that he would be able to buy his wife and two daughters at the auction block. If he even succeeded in purchasing them, he wasn't sure if he would be allowed to keep them. Slave owners were unpredictable when it came to free Africans purchasing their families. Kessiah, John, and their two small children, James and Araminta, were at terrible risk of never seeing each other again.

Harriet was quick to take action. She contacted the Vigilance Committee and told them that she wanted to act as a "conductor" for the little family. They helped to smuggle her down to Baltimore, Maryland, where she hid with John Tubman's brother Tom. Other conductors and stationmasters helped John Bowley, Kessiah, and the children to hide after the auction (John had managed to buy them after all).

Reaching Baltimore from the safe house was no mean feat, but the knowledge that her courageous, free Aunt Harriet was waiting for her on the other side helped Kessiah to hold on to hope as her husband desperately wrangled the little log canoe they were using to sail to the city. They made it in one piece, and Harriet welcomed them at once. She was a calm and courageous presence, and the family took hope in the fact that she had managed to make the journey to Pennsylvania once before. They knew that she could do it again.

And she did. Not only did she lead Kessiah's family to the free states, but she led them all the way to Ontario itself, where they could truly be free in the eyes of the law.

The feeling Harriet had as Kessiah and her family stepped across that border was something intoxicating. She knew that she had just achieved something glorious; she'd just given a new, free life to a little family that had known nothing but hardship. She believed in her heart then that she'd been literally heaven-sent to her beleaguered family back in Maryland. Instead of crossing into the safety of Ontario with John and Kessiah, Harriet decided that she had to help the rest of her family get there too. So, she turned around and headed back into the danger zone to set her people free, to lead them, one by one, to the Promised Land.

Rejected by John

It wasn't long before Harriet was back in Maryland, returning once again to the land she had fought so hard to escape from. This time, she'd gotten wind of the location of her younger brother Moses, the little boy that Rit had fought to keep from being sold out of her arms. Rit had long since lost contact with Moses, but somehow, Harriet found him. She had cared for him when he was just a baby, and now, she took his hand and led him to freedom, giving him the one gift that Rit had been unable to.

Harriet had now freed her niece and brother, as well as a few other unrelated people whose names have not been documented. She forged strong friendships with the abolitionists back in Philadelphia, working hand in hand with William Still and helping to develop a network of depots in Maryland. She also became close friends with Frederick Douglass. Douglass had become a stationmaster on the Underground Railroad himself, harboring around 400 fugitives during his time as stationmaster. He spoke of Harriet with only the highest praise. She was a hero of heroes.

As the winter of 1851 rolled around, Harriet prepared for another foray into Maryland. This time, she hoped to retrieve another family member: her own husband. Even though John Tubman was free, it would be difficult for him to escape to Pennsylvania in broad daylight since Southern whites resisted the migration of Africans to the free states. Harriet and John had a turbulent marriage, but he was still her husband. She'd made a vow to be loyal to him, and she intended to keep that vow, even though it meant another risky journey through slave owners' territory.

Harriet made the journey in late 1851. It was her first time returning to the county where she'd been born and raised, and she knew that there would be no hiding in plain sight. With her short stature (she was only around five feet tall), Harriet was easily recognizable. If Brodess's widow or Anthony Thompson Jr. saw her, she could end up right back in the chains that she was working so hard to liberate others from.

Yet she would not be cowed. Carrying the suit that she'd bought for her husband (John, as a poor temporary laborer, owned only rags; a ragged African man traveling without a white companion would arouse suspicion), Harriet made her way into Maryland. As soon as she could, she sent him a message, telling him that she'd come for him and that she was bringing him into the beautiful new life she'd built for herself. Things had been hard between Harriet and John, and she'd gone directly against his wishes by leaving Maryland. Yet she hoped that the promise of freedom would reunite them.

She was wrong. John let her know in no uncertain terms that he was happy where he was for a simple reason: he had remarried. Since he and Harriet were not legally married due to her legal status as an enslaved person, there had been no need to file for divorce. He'd just married a new woman and forgotten about Harriet, and he had no desire to come with her now.

Harriet was incensed. She had a good mind to charge over to John's house, break down his door, and drag him to Pennsylvania whether he liked it or not. But when she heard of another group of fugitives hiding out nearby—people who were actually desperate to get out of Maryland—she decided that he didn't deserve her help. She left him in Maryland, where he would die in a confrontation with another man a few years later, and met up with the eleven escapees instead.

Working with these people was a milestone for Harriet. Before this, she'd been focused on just bringing her family out of slavery and into Ontario. But when she met these eleven strangers, she became a true conductor of the Underground Railroad, someone who would lead anyone who needed help to find freedom.

By this time, she had already made numerous trips from Maryland to Ontario, and she was no frightened little fugitive anymore. Photographs of Harriet depict a short woman with a pinched face and the grim, determined expression of a warrior. Her eyes were filled with utter steel, and her firm conviction and clenched-jawed fearlessness still shine through in her images. She commanded instant respect from her charges.

Harriet saved people, but she could also be firm with them. She carried drugs to give to babies or small children if their crying threatened to give away their position. Escapees joining her noticed that she carried a revolver and that she knew how to use it. She fired on slave catchers whenever necessary, and when an escapee got cold feet, Harriet was not above drawing her weapon on them as well. She had been burned too badly by the betrayal of Ben and Henry back in 1849 to allow any of the fugitives she helped to return to their plantations and give away details about the Underground Railroad. Once fugitives began their journey with Harriet, they had no choice but to see it through all the way to Ontario. She never actually had to use her revolver on any of the escapees. Just the sight of those steely eyes behind the shiny little barrel was enough to convince any enslaved person that Harriet was not someone they wanted to anger. "You go on or die," she told them. They always went on. And they always reached Canada.

"I never lost a passenger," Harriet would later say proudly. Every person she ever left Maryland with made it to Ontario.

It was more than just her firm resolve that kept her passengers alive as they trekked through the winter landscape. Harriet's quick wit stood her in good stead, as she planned all kinds of tactics to keep her passengers hidden. Like other conductors on the Underground Railroad, she sent all of her messages in code. She also had other ways to communicate with passengers and stationmasters alike, such as mimicking bird calls or using songs with slightly altered lyrics or tempos. Her particular favorite was "Go Down Moses."

In the cool winter nights, as they cowered in the homes of the stationmasters with the knowledge that slave catchers were around every corner, escapees could hear Harriet's high voice carry through the air toward them. "So the Lord said, go down, Moses, way down in Egypt land; tell all the pharaohs to let My people go!"

The Southern slave owners didn't let their people go, but Harriet took them north anyway. She reached Frederick Douglass's house safely with the eleven people she'd rescued instead of her errant husband. Douglass cared for the fugitives for a time and raised funds to help them on the rest of their journey.

Harriet would return many times to Dorchester County specifically, despite the enormous risk. More than once, she encountered people who had formerly owned her and legally still did. She used various disguises to escape notice. One time, she held up a newspaper despite the fact that she never learned to read. Another time, she carried a pair of chickens as part of her disguise and pretended to be struggling to control them in order to hide her face.

On one occasion, Harriet would return to Dorchester County on a very special mission to rescue Ben Ross and Rit Green, her parents. Her mother had been a heroine and an inspiration to Harriet as a child, and even now, she continued to act with inspiring courage and determination. Because of her role as a cook for Edward Brodess's widow, Rit had not been sold when Edward died. Ben was manumitted at some point and was able to earn enough money to buy Rit. For a time, Harriet believed they were safe, but Ben and Rit weren't content with simply living a free life in Maryland. They became stationmasters themselves and harbored fugitive slaves, slipping them into the Railroad, of which their daughter had become its most famous conductor.

Ultimately, however, this almost led to their capture. Authorities in the South learned that Ben and Rit were sheltering numerous escapees in their home. However, before the couple could be arrested, their daughter came to Maryland to slip them out from under the noses of the slave owners. She took Ben, Rit, and eight other escapees from Maryland, seeing them off safely to the growing colony of Africans in Ontario. Harriet made her mother's greatest dream come true, and Rit lived out the rest of her life in freedom, surrounded by her vast family.

By then, Harriet's role as a conductor on the Underground Railroad had been firmly established. Until the start of the Civil War, she would make at least one trip every year, bringing people from Maryland to Canada. As each person crossed the border into Ontario, she would cry out in delight, "Glory to God and Jesus too. One more soul is safe!"

She would repeat this refrain around seventy times: that was roughly the number of verified people that Harriet personally brought to Canada. Who knows how many more benefited from the growing network of depots and stationmasters that she helped to build in Maryland? She made the perilous journey to Maryland around thirteen times, making her one of the most successful and hardworking conductors of the Underground Railroad. Her efforts earned her the nickname of "the Moses of her people," and just like that biblical prophet, she led refugees to freedom in a new land.

Chapter 6 – More Heroes of the Underground Railroad

The Gateway to Freedom sculpture in Detroit, Michigan, is a monument to many of the abolitionists who saved enslaved people via the Underground Railroad.

Ken Lund from Las Vegas, Nevada, USA, CC BY-SA 2.0
<https://creativecommons.org/licenses/by-sa/2.0>, via Wikimedia Commons
https://commons.wikimedia.org/wiki/File:Gateway_to_Freedom_sculpture,_Hart_Plaza,_Det roit,_Michigan_(14224050363).jpg

While William Still was the father of the Underground Railroad, and Harriet Tubman its most well-known conductor, this network of heroes was by no means limited to only one or two people. Every single person who worked on the Railroad contributed to saving over 100,000 people from slavery.

To tell all of their stories would take thousands of books. We will explore a few of the most well known, starting with the stationmaster who possibly sheltered more people than any other: Jermain Loguen.

The King of the Underground Railroad

Jarm Logue was born on February 5th, 1813, and he was of mixed race. However, his parents were no doting interracial couple. His mother, Cherry, was an enslaved woman, and like so many other enslaved women, she had to serve her master in any way he chose—even if that included giving up her body to him. To deny her owner his perceived "right" to do with his "property" however he pleased meant facing terrible physical punishment. Cherry submitted to her owner, David Logue, and the result was a little boy, whom she named Jarm.

Cherry was determined that little Jarm wouldn't have to suffer the same dreadful treatment to which she had been subjected all her life. In 1834, a year after the British Empire had abolished slavery, Cherry plotted twenty-one-year-old Jarm's escape. Now that there was a free country he could go to, Cherry resolved not to allow her son to live out his life in bondage.

She herself would remain behind in David Logue's service, but her attempt to help her young son go free was a successful one. They took Logue's horse out of the stable in the dead of night, and Jarm climbed up into the saddle. Although riding wasn't something that enslaved people were taught how to do, he knew he would just have to figure it out as he went along. He kissed his mother goodbye and rode off into the night. And he rode all the way to St. Catherine's, Ontario, a popular settlement for escapees.

Jarm wouldn't stay in Ontario for long. Even though he was safer there, he returned to New York to study at the Oneida Institute, the first college in the United States to freely admit African students. Here, he became literate and studied theology.

In 1840, he moved to Syracuse, New York, to become a minister there. He had married a girl named Caroline and changed his name to Jermain Wesley Loguen in honor of the leader of the Methodist Revival, John Wesley. Here, Loguen would purchase a piece of property and start his lifelong mission to protect people who were escaping from slavery, just as he had.

Over the next twenty-three years, Jermain and Caroline would dedicate their lives to helping people out of slavery. He became a key part of the Underground Railroad in New York. He constructed numerous buildings on his land that were solely designed to accommodate escapees, even adding bunks into the basement of his own house to shelter as many enslaved people as possible. Caroline would provide escapees with food and a hot bath, things that were much-needed after so many weary miles on the road. Loguen would encourage them with his religious training, and they would be sent on their way to Canada with clean clothes, full bellies, rested feet, and warmed hearts.

In total, Jermain and Caroline Loguen would help around 1,500 escapees along the Underground Railroad. This vast number earned them the nicknames of the King and Queen of the Underground Railroad. They were fearlessly open about their role as Underground Railroad stationmasters and would also speak up constantly for the abolitionist cause. Jermain even authored a popular slave narrative detailing his life in bondage and his escape. The Loguens were close friends with the Douglass family. In 1869, when the dust had settled after the Civil War, their daughter married one of Frederick Douglass's sons. Their other daughter, Sarah Loguen Fraser, was one of the first female African American doctors.

Gerrit Smith

While many Underground Railroad heroes came from hard childhoods or even from slavery themselves, one notable stationmaster couldn't have had a more different childhood from someone like Jermain Loguen or Harriet Tubman.

Gerrit Smith was born in 1797 into one of New York's wealthiest families. His father, Peter Smith, had built a little town called Peterboro, where Gerrit grew up. The Smiths were old money, and young Gerrit wanted for nothing. While the likes of John Brown and Frederick Douglass were spending back-breaking hours in plantation fields, Gerrit Smith was getting an education and learning how to mingle with high society.

Nonetheless, Smith was an abolitionist to his very core, and he would become an integral part of not only the Underground Railroad but of the abolitionist movement as a whole. He was already interested in abolition in 1835 when he attended a conference hosted by the Utica Anti-Slavery Society. Utica was a small town in Oneida County, New York. Unfortunately, the conference was ill-fated. While over 600 abolitionists had gathered to discuss the issue of abolition and of the Fugitive Slave Act, 80 anti-abolitionists rioted and attacked the church where the conference was being held. The conference was in danger of being completely canceled when Smith, inspired by the cause, stepped up and offered to host it in Peterboro instead. The Anti-Slavery Society was so impressed by his actions that he was elected president the following year. He would serve until 1839, by which time he had traveled to the South and been deeply affected by the brutality he witnessed there. He started to ignore the fugitive slave laws and encouraged the other members of the society to do the same.

After his stint as president of the Anti-Slavery Society, Smith began to get more hands-on when it came to abolition, as he became a stationmaster of the Underground Railroad. His vast estate was easy for escapees to find, and it could accommodate vast numbers of refugees, who were often given significant financial aid during their stay on Smith's estate. Some would continue on to Canada with more than enough money to make their way there and even start a new life; others, however, chose to settle in New York itself. One of Smith's projects was to sell small farms to people who had once been enslaved. These farms were not only homes but also opportunities to open businesses and create a living for people who had fled from slavery without a penny to their names. He would sell the farms to these ex-slaves, charging them only a single dollar for each piece of land. About 140,000 acres were distributed in this way, assisting more than 3,000 escapees.

Over the years, Smith pumped millions of dollars into the abolitionist cause, from funding clandestine activities to buying the freedom of enslaved people to supporting various abolitionist publications. He was close friends with Frederick Douglass and often provided funding for the latter's newspaper, aptly named *The North Star* after the star that thousands of escapees followed during their nightly journeys out of bondage. He became a source of much of the Underground Railroad's finances, with thousands upon thousands of his dollars feeding, clothing, educating, and transporting escapees. Smith also spent his money in the South, buying up whole families of enslaved people at a time only to bring them to the North and legally grant them their freedom. They were then spared the trip to Canada, and they were able to settle comfortably in the North, secure in the knowledge that Smith's actions had made them as legally free as he was.

In total, Smith gave away around eight million dollars to various causes, which equals to around a quarter of a billion dollars today. He died peacefully in 1874, having seen slavery abolished throughout the United States.

The Mercenary Conductor

Another figure of the Underground Railroad who was also born into privilege was John Fairfield. While he was not as influential, rich, or in possession of as fine-tuned a moral compass as Gerrit Smith, he was certainly a very interesting character.

John Fairfield was born in Virginia as the son of wealthy slave owners. He led a privileged life that differed greatly from that of his childhood best friend, a little boy who was enslaved by Fairfield's uncle. As a child, Fairfield couldn't understand why his friend led a life so different from his own. While Fairfield slept on a feather bed and had a full-time governess, his enslaved friend slept on the dirt floor of a hovel and never had the chance to even learn his alphabet. Fairfield ate every delicacy he wanted, but his friend never knew the luxury of a full belly. Yet, in Fairfield's eyes, his enslaved friend was every bit as human as he was himself.

Fairfield and the enslaved boy grew up side by side despite the vast gulf between them socially; somehow, their friendship knew nothing of their legal divide. It was inevitable, however, that adulthood would separate them. Fairfield was a young man (it is unclear exactly when he was born) when the selfish will of his friend's owner threatened to tear them apart.

If Fairfield had been any ordinary slave owner's son, he would have watched his friend go, perhaps with some tears, and then gotten on with his privileged life. But this young man was no ordinary person. He had a depth of courage and a sense of justice to complement his fiery nature, and when he learned that his friend was going to be sold, that sense of justice was truly offended. It was brutally brought home to him that slavery was not the "benevolent institution" that his family had always told him it was. He decided that the only way to save his friend was to help him escape slavery entirely. (This points to the fact that Fairfield was likely a teenager at this time, as if he was an adult, he would have been able to buy his friend from his uncle and thus set him free.)

The escape itself was not as hard as it had been for Harriet Tubman or Frederick Douglass. For a young, wealthy white man, to move across the South accompanied by someone who appeared to be enslaved was a cakewalk. No one gave them a second glance. It wasn't long before Fairfield's friend was delivered safely into the free states, and Fairfield himself was on his way back home, satisfied with his little escapade.

However, when he got there, he found that he was no longer welcome. His uncle, the owner of his newly freed friend, had found out that it was his young nephew who had facilitated the enslaved boy's escape. He put a price on Fairfield's head. Fairfield had given up his own liberty for that of his friend.

To a hot-blooded young man like Fairfield, the solution was simple. He sneaked onto his uncle's land, saddled his horses, put his enslaved people on their backs, and led them all to freedom in the dead of night. And so began the career of the Underground Railroad's most colorful and swashbuckling conductor.

Fairfield's stint as a conductor took place in the 1850s, when the Fugitive Slave Act of 1850 had made the Underground Railroad more important than ever. He was well known to the likes of Coffin, Still, and Douglass, but they saw him as something of a nuisance at best and someone frankly dangerous and immoral at worst. Fairfield lacked the pureness of heart displayed by other abolitionists. He was something of a mercenary conductor, as he often charged money from the already penniless escapees in exchange for his services in retrieving their family members from slavery. Levi Coffin called him a "snake." But although he was unconventional, there is no denying that Fairfield was effective. In his ten years as a conductor, he rescued several thousand enslaved people, many of them from states in the Deep South that were unreachable for the likes of Tubman.

Even Fairfield's methods were unorthodox. He delighted in elaborate plots involving extensive role-play, often posing as a slave owner and even organizing searches for his "runaway slaves" to lead slave catchers off in one direction while escapees fled in another. Once, he hid about twenty-six people in plain sight by organizing them in a funeral procession, including hiding one man in the coffin itself. They rode right through a Kentucky town, over the river, and off to freedom before anyone could stop them.

As he'd demonstrated by the theft of his uncle's horses, Fairfield was not above lining his pockets during these missions. He often made off not only with enslaved people but also with jewels and money. Although many abolitionists despised him for his mercenary ways, these thefts profited escapees, as Fairfield gave most of his "proceeds" to the growing colony of runaways at the Elgin Settlement in Ontario.

Ultimately, Fairfield may have been a rogue in life, but he proved his true dedication to the cause of abolitionism in his violent death. John Fairfield went missing sometime shortly before the Civil War. It is now thought that he died fighting for the freedom of the people that his family had enslaved, for a young man of similar description is recorded as being killed during a Tennessee rebellion of enslaved people in 1860. Fairfield may have been leading the rebellion himself.

Either way, even Coffin, a long-time hater of Fairfield, had to concede that for all his faults, the hot-headed young conductor was "a brave man" and "a true friend to the oppressed and suffering slave."

John Brown and the League of Gileadites

If Harriet Tubman was the Moses of her people, John Brown considered himself their Joshua.

Tubman had been ready to shoot if necessary; Brown was trigger-happy. As the 1850s dragged on, unrest grew across the United States as it barreled toward the Civil War. While most members of the Underground Railroad still sought a peaceful path to abolition, some believed from the start that war was inevitable. The most controversial of them all was John Brown. Widely known for his raid on Harper's Ferry, which has long been considered a precursor for the American

Civil War, Brown was, in many ways, idealistic, but he was also a violent man whose thirst for justice often overwhelmed his respect for human life. Yet it's a little-known fact that Brown himself was one of the Underground Railroad's most successful stationmasters.

Brown was a second-generation member of the Underground Railroad. Born on May 9th, 1800, in Connecticut, Brown was of English descent and born into freedom but also into abolitionism. His father, Owen Brown, was a stationmaster for the early Underground Railroad during John's childhood in Hudson, Ohio. Brown grew up looking into the frightened, drawn faces of escapees and hearing the shocking stories of their suffering at the hands of slave owners and catchers. He became a more conscious abolitionist thanks to the tutor he had in his teenage years, who was profoundly abolitionist.

Still, Brown's first choice of career was not as a violent activist. Instead, he studied to be a minister for several years until Owen, who was a poor tanner, could no longer afford Brown's tuition. Instead, the young man started up a tannery of his own on the outskirts of Hudson, and like his father, he started to take in fugitive slaves as soon as possible.

For Brown, though, the cause of abolitionism would take over his entire life. In 1825, he and his first wife, Dianthe, decided to move to New Richmond in Pennsylvania. This was a place many escapees fled to as they crossed the border from Maryland, and the Browns believed they could help more escapees by moving here. They were right. Over the next ten years, Brown worked as an outstanding stationmaster, assisted first by Dianthe and later by his very young second wife, Mary Ann, whom he married in 1833 when she was only sixteen. Dianthe had died a year earlier in 1832.

In those ten years, Brown was no controversial figure. He was simply a hero to those hoping to escape slavery. His depot was a sanctuary of peace, a beloved stepping stone to freedom for thousands of slaves; in fact, around 2,500 people owed their freedom at least in part to John Brown and his family.

His Underground Railroad activities likely continued into the 1840s, but a series of events would gradually drive Brown into a bitterness that ultimately turned gruesomely violent. In 1837, Elijah P. Lovejoy, an abolitionist, was murdered by pro-slavery elements during a riot. His death affected Brown deeply. From that moment onward, thirty-seven-year-old Brown's life was absolutely dedicated to abolitionism—he even swore an oath that he would not rest until he had seen slavery abolished.

By 1842, his new focus on abolitionism spelled disaster for the successful business he had been running. He declared bankruptcy, and the following year, he lost not one but four of his children to a dysentery outbreak. Three years later, he moved to Springfield, Massachusetts, a deeply abolitionist community that would influence him powerfully. It was here that he came into contact with abolitionist heroes, such as Harriet Tubman and Frederick Douglass. Both of them hoped for a peaceful resolution to the issue of slavery, yet both of them admired Brown for his unending commitment to the cause.

In 1850, sparked by the Fugitive Slave Act, Brown took his first step toward the violence that would characterize the remainder of his abolitionist career with the formation of the League of Gileadites. Where the Underground Railroad was the equivalent of Moses leading the Israelites to freedom, the League of Gileadites was equated with the assembly of the Israelites' bravest warriors in order to do battle for the Promise Land. It was, simply put, a militant organization. And it would shed much blood in the years to come.

Bleeding Kansas erupted in 1855. New states in the West, such as Kansas, were allowed to vote on whether they wanted to be slave or free states—a sudden departure from the sharp geographical boundary that used to divide the free North from the slavery-fueled South. Citizens of Kansas blew up into a period of rioting and violence that would take many lives. Brown and his League had a hand in some of those killings. During the Pottawatomie massacre in 1856, Brown and several of his associates attacked and killed five unarmed pro-slavery activists.

Things famously came to a head for Brown and for the United States of America in October 1859. For two long decades, Brown had been planning military action against the slave owners. He was firmly convinced that there was no use in persuading slave owners to give up their human possessions. Many other famous abolitionists, including Harriet Tubman, whose commanding presence and ability as a strategist earned her the nickname of "General Tubman" from Brown, were involved in planning the raid. However, there is evidence that many of them had doubts about the plan.

Brown had no doubts at all. In his mind, only bloodshed would result in freedom. He began that bloodshed on October 16th, 1859, launching a raid on the military outpost at Harper's Ferry, West Virginia. His first goal was to take the armory there and hold it against the United States Army, which was then still united. His second goal was to kidnap a local slave owner named Lewis Washington, who was a descendant of America's very first president. The Washington family still owned enslaved people.

The kidnapping was successful. The capturing of the armory was only briefly so. And the raid itself was an appalling failure. The first casualty of them all was an innocent railroad worker, a free African American, who failed to get out of Brown's way in time and received a bullet to the back for his trouble. Over the next few days, many more people died, including one of Brown's sons. John Brown quickly and bloodily learned that his little force of twenty-three men couldn't stand against the might of the US Army, which marched against him, surrounded him where he dug into the fort at Harper's Ferry, and ultimately killed or captured every last one of his men.

Brown was tried for treason and hanged for his crimes on December 2nd, 1859. His raid on Harper's Ferry would go down in history as a dress rehearsal for the bloodiest war in American history.

For John Brown was right after all. Only blood could ultimately buy freedom.

Conclusion

The Underground Railroad remained in operation until 1862, right in the midst of the American Civil War. When that time came, it was by no means the end of abolitionists' activities when it came to helping people escape from slavery. The Railroad still existed; it was just no longer "underground." When Lincoln signed the Emancipation Proclamation, it gave abolitionists permission to start working openly to free all enslaved people.

The heroes in this book who survived until the Civil War all served an important role in the war itself. Gerrit Smith spoke of peace during the devastating war; he even reached out to Southerners with compassion and helped to pay the bail bond for the Confederate's ill-fated president, Jefferson Davis. Harriet Tubman became the first African American woman to lead a military action. She exchanged her little revolver for a sharpshooter's rifle and led raids during the Civil War, freeing thousands more enslaved people.

Frederick Douglass was close with Abraham Lincoln during the Civil War, and after it, he became a highly-ranked government official, the first African American man to hold such a high position in the United States. He even met and forgave his erstwhile owner, Thomas Auld.

William Still managed a boot camp for the Union Army near his beloved city of Philadelphia. Even after the war, he continued to be a dedicated philanthropist, with a particular heart for children of color.

Ultimately, all of their efforts would pay off. The American Civil War started in 1861, and the Union Army won at last in the spring of 1865. With that victory, slavery was abolished throughout the entire United States of America. Liberty had been won at last, but it came at a terrible cost. Around 620,000 to perhaps over a million soldiers perished in that war. About 40,000 were African Americans, runaway slaves, or free soldiers who had joined the cause of liberating their brethren in bondage.

The fight against slavery had been won at last, but the fight for racial equality still rages on to this very day. Racial injustice continues in the United States and in the world at large, and considering that it has been nearly 200 years since the likes of John Brown first became stationmasters and conductors of the Underground Railroad, it is easy to be demoralized by the fact that we have still not managed to root out the idea that skin color has some kind of bearing on a human being's importance.

Yet looking at the story of the Underground Railroad, we can glean one thing from the determination and courage of these abolitionist heroes: hope. For where there was slavery in the British Empire, there was Thomas Clarkson and William Wilberforce. Where there was slavery among the Quakers, there was Benjamin Lay. Where there was slavery in the South, there was Harriet Tubman and John Fairfield.

And where there is inequality today, where there is prejudice, where there is racism, where there is injustice, there are heroes who will rise against it.

Here's another book by Captivating History that you might like

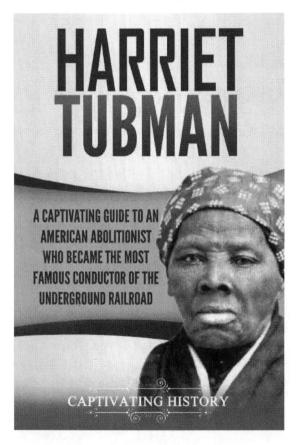

Free Bonus from Captivating History
(Available for a Limited time)

Hi History Lovers!

Now you have a chance to join our exclusive history list so you can get your first history ebook for free as well as discounts and a potential to get more history books for free! Simply visit the link below to join.

Captivatinghistory.com/ebook

Also, make sure to follow us on Facebook, Twitter and Youtube by searching for Captivating History.

Sources

Lewis, T. 2020, *Transatlantic Slave Trade*, Encyclopedia Britannica, viewed 3 November 2020, <https://www.britannica.com/topic/transatlantic-slave-trade>

Bortolot, A. I. 2003, *Women Leaders in African History: Ana Nzinga, Queen of Ndongo*, The Met Museum, viewed 3 November 2020, <https://www.metmuseum.org/toah/hd/pwmn_2/hd_pwmn_2.htm>

Understanding Slavery 2019, *Africa Before Transatlantic Enslavement*, Black History Month, viewed 3 November 2020, <https://www.blackhistorymonth.org.uk/article/section/history-of-slavery/africa-before-transatlantic-enslavement/>

Elliot, M. 2019, *A Brief History of Slavery That You Didn't Learn in School*, The New York Times Magazine, viewed 3 November 2020, <https://www.nytimes.com/interactive/2019/08/19/magazine/history-slavery-smithsonian.html>

Restavek Freedom 2018, *The History of Slavery*, Restavek Freedom, viewed 3 November 2020, <https://restavekfreedom.org/2018/09/11/the-history-of-slavery/>

Africans in America: A Life of Slavery, Library of Congress, viewed 3 November 2020, <https://www.loc.gov/classroom-materials/immigration/african/africans-in-america/>

USHistory.org 2020, *Slave Life and Slave Codes*, U. S. History Online Textbook, viewed 12 November 2020, <https://www.ushistory.org/us/27b.asp>

National Geographic Society 2019, *Abolition and the Abolitionists*, National Geographic, viewed 17 November 2020, <https://www.nationalgeographic.org/encyclopedia/abolition-and-abolitionists/>

The Editors of the Encyclopedia Britannica 2019, *Abolitionism*, Encyclopedia Britannica, viewed 17 November 2020, <https://www.britannica.com/topic/abolitionism-European-and-American-social-movement>

Huzzey, R. 2016, *Development and the abolitionist movement in history*, Anti-Slavery, viewed 17 November 2020, <https://www.antislavery.org/development-abolitionist-movement-history/>

Quakers in the World, *Anti-Slavery*, Quakers in the World, viewed 17 November 2020, <https://www.quakersintheworld.org/quakers-in-action/11/-Anti-Slavery>

Rediker, M. 2017, *The "Quaker Comet" was the Greatest Abolitionist You've Never Heard Of*, Smithsonian Magazine, viewed 17 November 2020, <https://www.smithsonianmag.com/history/quaker-comet-greatest-abolitionist-never-heard-180964401/>

BBC 2014, *Granville Sharp (1735-1813)*, British Broadcasting Commission, viewed 17 November 2020, <http://www.bbc.co.uk/history/historic_figures/sharp_granville.shtml>

Jarus, O. 2019, *What Was the Enlightenment?*, Live Science, viewed 17 November 2020, <https://www.livescience.com/55327-the-enlightenment.html>

Galli, M. and Olsen, T. with Christian History Magazine 2000, *131 Christians Everyone Should Know*, Holman Reference, accessed at Christianity Today, 17 November 2020, <https://www.christianitytoday.com/history/people/activists/william-wilberforce.html> <https://www.christianitytoday.com/history/people/activists/harriet-tubman.html>

BBC 2014, *Thomas Clarkson (1760-1846)*, British Broadcasting Commission, viewed 17 November 2020, <http://www.bbc.co.uk/history/historic_figures/clarkson_thomas.shtml>

Histoy.com Editors, *Nat Turner*, A&E Television Networks, viewed 17 November 2020, <https://www.history.com/topics/black-history/nat-turner>

Deibert, B. 2018, *Who Are the Quakers?*, Christianity.com, viewed 17 November 2020, <https://www.christianity.com/church/denominations/the-quakers-7-things-about-their-history-beliefs.html>

Biography.com Editors 2020, *Frederick Douglass Biography*, A&E Television Networks, viewed 18 November 2020, <https://www.biography.com/activist/frederick-douglass>

Russell, T. 2020, *Still, William*, Encyclopedia of African-American Culture and History, viewed 18 November 2020, <https://www.encyclopedia.com/history/historians-and-chronicles/historians-miscellaneous-biographies/william-still>

Caust-Ellenbogen, C. 2009, *Isaac T. Hopper*, Quakers & Slavery, viewed 18 November 2020, <https://web.tricolib.brynmawr.edu/speccoll/quakersandslavery/commentary/people/hopper.php>

History.com Editors 2020, *Fugitive Slave Acts*, A&E Television Networks, viewed 18 November 2020, <https://www.history.com/topics/black-history/fugitive-slave-acts>

Biography.com Editors 2019, *Henry Clay Biography*, A&E Television Networks, viewed 18 November 2020, <https://www.biography.com/political-figure/henry-clay>

Hagen, C. 2020, *The Courageous Tale of Jane Johnson, Who Risked Her Freedom for Those Who Helped Her Escape Slavery*, Smithsonian Magazine, viewed 18 November 2020, <https://www.smithsonianmag.com/history/courageous-tale-jane-johnson-who-risked-her-freedom-testify-those-who-helped-her-escape-180976302/>

Chang, R. 2019, *How Harriet Tubman and William Still Helped the Underground Railroad*, A&E Television Networks, viewed 21 November 2020, <https://www.biography.com/news/harriet-tubman-william-still-helped-slaves-escape-underground-railroad>

Michals, D. 2015, *Harriet Tubman*, National Women's History Magazine, viewed 21 November 2020, <https://www.womenshistory.org/education-resources/biographies/harriet-tubman>

Shoot, B. 2020, *The Brain Injury That Helped End Slavery*, Folks, viewed 21 November 2020, <https://folks.pillpack.com/brain-injury-helped-end-slavery/>

Ishak, N. 2019, *Inside the Life of John Tubman, Harriet's Husband Who Didn't Follow Her North*, All That's Interesting, viewed 21 November 2020, <https://allthatsinteresting.com/john-tubman>

The Editors of Encyclopedia Britannica 2020, *Harriet Tubman*, Encyclopedia Britannica, viewed 21 November 2020, <https://www.britannica.com/biography/Harriet-Tubman>

History.com Editors 2020, *Harriet Tubman*, A&E Television Networks, viewed 21 November 2020, <https://www.history.com/topics/black-history/harriet-tubman>

Simkin, J. 2014, *Slavery in the United States*, Spartacus Educational Publishers

Kate Clifford Larsen's Harriet Tubman Biography website: http://harriettubmanbiography.com/

History.com Editors 2020, *John Brown*, A&E Television Networks, viewed 21 November 2020, <https://www.history.com/topics/abolitionist-movement/john-brown>

Copeland, J. S. 2014, *Ain't No Harm to Kill the Devil: The Life and Legend of John Fairfield, Abolitionist for Hire*, Paragon House

Dann, N. K., *Gerrit Smith*, National Abolition Hall of Fame and Museum, viewed 21 November 2020, <https://www.nationalabolitionhalloffameandmuseum.org/gerrit-smith.html>

Engledew, D. 2007, *Jermain Wesley Loguen (1813-1872)*, Black Past, viewed 21 November 2020, <https://www.blackpast.org/african-american-history/loguen-jermain-wesley-1813-1872/>

Bordewich, F. M. 2009, *John Brown's Day of Reckoning*, Smithsonian Magazine, viewed 21 November 2020, <https://www.smithsonianmag.com/history/john-browns-day-of-reckoning-139165084/>

Encyclopedia of World Biography, *Levi Coffin*, Encyclopedia.com, viewed 21 November 2020, <https://www.encyclopedia.com/people/social-sciences-and-law/social-reformers/levi-coffin>

Editors of the Encyclopedia Britannica 2020, *Levi Coffin*, Encyclopedia Britannica, viewed 21 November 2020, <https://www.britannica.com/biography/Levi-Coffin>

History.com Editors 2019, *Underground Railroad*, A&E Television Networks, viewed 21 November 2020, <https://www.history.com/topics/black-history/underground-railroad#section_6>

History.com Editors 2020, *Slavery in America*, A&E Television Networks, viewed 21 November 2020, <https://www.history.com/topics/black-history/slavery#section_6>

Illustrations:

Illustration I:
https://commons.wikimedia.org/wiki/File:Ann_Zingha.jpg

Illustration II:
https://commons.wikimedia.org/wiki/File:Benjamin_Lay_painted_by_William_Williams_in_1790.jpg

Illustration III:
https://upload.wikimedia.org/wikipedia/commons/a/a9/Levi_coffin.JPG

Public Domain,
https://commons.wikimedia.org/w/index.php?curid=81617527

Illustration V: By Ken Lund from Las Vegas, Nevada, USA - The Gateway to Freedom, Hart Plaza, Detroit, Michigan, CC BY-SA 2.0, https://commons.wikimedia.org/w/index.php?curid=41846197

Made in the USA
Las Vegas, NV
26 July 2024

92994726R00061